PRECISION BIDDING AND
PRECISION PLAY

PRECISION BIDDING AND
PRECISION PLAY

FOUR YEARS AGO A BOMBSHELL EXPLODED
IN THE WORLD OF TOURNAMENT BRIDGE
when a team from Nationalist China, chosen from a few
hundred enthusiasts, finished second to Italy in the world
championship. The team were playing a new bidding
system called 'Precision', devised by the multi-millionaire
C. C. Wei.

The initial success for the system was soon followed by
many more, and players throughout the world have
turned to Precision, hoping for an improvement in their
bidding. To guide them, they have depended on a number
of books, but none of these expound the System in sufficient detail to deal effectively with the many tricky situations which arise in tournament bridge. It was clear that
the British, Italian and American teams who were playing
Precision so successfully had polished the System in a way
not described in any book. This situation has now been
rectified by the publication of Terence Reese's *Precision
Bidding and Precision Play*. This book explains and considers
in depth every bidding situation which is likely to occur
and whole chapters are devoted to single themes. In other
words, here is a definitive account of the system, and
pairs playing Precision are no longer thrown back on
their own initiative in various sequences. To my mind,
Terence Reese is by far the best living writer on bridge
and this book in every way lives up to his usual high
standard.

LEWIS R. GRITTIN in the *South Wales Evening Argus*

PRECISION BIDDING AND PRECISION PLAY

Terence Reese

Introduction by C. C. Wei

A STAR BOOK
published by
W. H. ALLEN

A Star Book
Published in 1974
by W. H. Allen & Co. Ltd.
A division of Howard & Wyndham Ltd,
44 Hill Street, London W1X 8LB

First published in Great Britain by
W. H. Allen Ltd. 1972

Printed in Great Britain by
Richard Clay (The Chaucer Press), Ltd., Bungay, Suffolk

ISBN 0 352 30013 2

CONTENTS

INTRODUCTION

I hardly need to introduce the great Terence Reese; it is much more fitting that he should introduce me. As, in this book, indeed he has.

Unlike most inventors of bridge systems, I never claimed to be the world's greatest player. I claim only the greatest love and admiration for the game. In fact, when I first began to think about a bridge system, it was with the aim of making contract bridge as popular as football in Europe or baseball in the United States. Indeed, my first contact with an expert of top rank came through calling him up and inviting him to be my guest at a World Series game in Yankee Stadium. There I got some wise but painful advice. The idea I was working on wasn't new, had not been successful, and was not acceptable to the average player. So, I scrapped my plan to have the first two bids exchange precise information about point-count holdings and, being an engineer by training, went back to the drawing-board.

It took almost five years to produce the Precision system, in which my idea of showing strength with the first bids was combined with the equally important objective of having almost all bids retain their natural meaning.

Frankly, my primary goal was to produce a system that would make bidding easier for the average player and at the same time produce better results. It was not until my 'average player' friends began to do consistently well in competition with experts that I knew that, while achieving my principal goal of simplicity, I had also fashioned a method that could succeed even at the highest levels of play.

The first players to become convinced were my fellow-Chinese. Using the Precision system, they jolted the world's top experts to attention by finishing second to the great Italian Blue Team in the 1969 world championship for the Bermuda Bowl. Then, to prove it was no fluke, my underdog Republic of China team again won the runner-up spot in the 1970 world championship, losing only to Ira Corn's top professional team, the Aces.

Meanwhile, some of the better American players became persuaded of the merits of Precision. The story of how a team of 'unknowns' won the National Team Championship for the Spingold Trophy in 1970 is quite amusing. One day Tom Smith, a young man on the staff of the American Contract Bridge League, rang me up and asked if I would mind if he and his friends played Precision in their next tournament. I said, 'Of course not, but to be fair to yourselves and to me you must do some training under my supervision'. I had had a good deal of experience, with my Chinese friends, in training methods, and I made sure that Steve Altman's team (he was the captain) would at least know what they were doing. Nobody thought of including this team among the sixteen seeds, but they came right through the field to win. Next year the story was 'As holders, we've got to put them among the top four, but it'll upset the whole seeding'. Well, believe it or not, they won again! To clinch the point, they went on to win the prized Vanderbilt Cup and the Spring 1972 Knockout Team Championship. This feat gave them a two out of two verdict against the world champion Aces and a phenomenal three wins out of four in successive national team events.

Elsewhere in the world great players took note until even the famous Blue Team itself, perennial world champions until their temporary retirement in 1969, changed from using three different methods and adopted Precision as their official system on their return to world competition in 1972.

Now, not the least of Precision's triumphs is that is has won the endorsement of Terence Reese, England's great authority on the game and perhaps today's greatest bridge writer. I am proud indeed that he has elected to present Precision.

As always, he has written a clear, thorough and authoritative book. I know you will find it fascinating. And, when you begin to follow his advice, I think you will find that Precision helps you to bid and play better – and with greater pleasure than ever before.

C. C. WEI
New York, April 1972

AUTHOR'S NOTE

When I wrote a series of articles on (simplified) Precision for the London *Evening News* I attached a point of play to many of the example hands. The idea seemed to be popular, so I have retained it here, justifying the book's title.

All the members of the British Precision team (Jeremy Flint, Jonathan Cansino, Robert Sheehan, Chris Dixon, Irving Rose, and myself) have contributed suggestions to this book. The principal theorist of our group is Jeremy Flint; in particular, the schemes for 5-card majors and sputnik doubles are in line with the ideas developed in his ferocious *Tiger Bridge*.

1 STRUCTURE OF THE SYSTEM

Broadly speaking, bidding systems fall into one of two groups: the approach-forcing systems, which include standard American and Acol, and the one club systems, which include the Vanderbilt club, the Ingram club, the Nottingham club, the Neapolitan club, the Schenken club, and now the Precision club. Thus there is nothing new in systems that use 1♣ as the standard opening for strong hands, and I don't want to start off on the wrong foot with readers by suggesting that Precision is some new and devilish weapon. What can fairly be said is that, following its initial successes, Precision has attracted the keenest minds on both sides of the Atlantic, and the version I present in this book fulfils, I believe, two standards: it is a method that is both easily learned and easy to play; and it forms an integrated system, worked out in sufficient detail to be adopted in tournament play at the highest level.

There have, of course, been previous accounts of Precision, mostly published in America. These books were designed to attract a big public and tended, perhaps, to oversimplify the system and to skate over the difficult areas of bidding. I have tried to avoid that, and a necessary consequence has been that many sequences and understandings are proposed that are not to be found in any of the earlier accounts. At the same time I have not tampered, if that is the right word, with the basic structure. All the opening bids have the same sense as in C. C. Wei's original summary.

Precision is basically a one club system with a weak notrump throughout and 5-card majors. These are the main opening sequences:

Opening bid

Opening bid	
1♣	Conventional, 16 upwards. **Responses:** 1◇ 0–7; 1♡ 1♠ 2♣ 2◇ positive, 8 upwards, with a 5-card suit; 1NT 8–10; 2♡ 2♠ semi-positive, 3–6; 2NT 11–13; 3♣ 3◇ 7-card suit with two top honours; 3♡ 3♠ 4–6, long suit; 3NT 14–15.
1◇	12–15, often a 3-card suit. Raise to 2◇ stronger than a raise to 3◇, other responses natural.
1♡ 1♠	12–15, 5-card suit in principle. Response of 1NT forcing for one round.
1NT	13–15 throughout. Response of 2♣ non-forcing Stayman, 2◇ forcing Stayman.
2♣	12–15, fair suit, may include a 4-card major. **Responses:** 2◇ conventional and forcing, 2♡ 2♠ invitational, 2NT natural, 3♣ constructive.
2◇	3-suiter or semi-3-suiter with short diamonds, 12–15.
2♡ 2♠	Weak two bid, 7–10 with a good suit. Response of 2NT conventional and forcing.
2NT	22–23, response of 3♣ Baron.
3♣	Strong suit, at least one stopper outside, 13–15.
3◇ 3♡ 3♠	Normal pre-empts.
3NT	Solid 7-card minor suit, no outside strength.
4♣ 4◇	Transfer bids for 4♡ and 4♠ respectively.
4♡ 4♠	Normal pre-empts.

2 THE OPENING 1♣ AND THE SYSTEM OF RESPONSES

Whether a newcomer to Precision should begin by studying the opening 1♣ is perhaps open to question, in an instructional sense. However, I feel that the student will want to meet something new and fresh, and as 1♣ happens also to be the lowest bid in the auction it seems a fair place to begin. All the remaining opening bids are treated in ascending sequence, which at least will make for ease of reference.

Except that 2NT is opened on balanced hands of 22-23 points, all hands of 16 upwards are opened with 1♣.

Having said that, it is necessary to comment on the status and relevance of valuation by point count. As no doubt all readers are aware, in the standard point count an ace is counted as 4 points, a king as 3, a queen as 2, a jack as 1. The point count is no more, and no less, than a convenient way of summarizing a hand in terms of its high cards. It is quicker to say 'an average hand contains 10 points' than to say 'an average hand contains an ace, a king, a queen and a jack'. When one says that all hands of 16 upwards are opened with 1♣, what one means is that an analysis of minimum hands suitable for 1♣ would reveal that their high-card strength averaged about 16. Obviously ♠A K J 10 7 4 ♥A Q J 6 3 ◇4 3 ♣— is a much more powerful hand than ♠K Q ♥8 7 6 4 2 ◇K Q J 4 ♣A J, though the first hand adds up to 15 and the second to 16. The reader should at no time feel that the number of points *dictates* the bid. As I remarked in an earlier book, the player who argues along the lines 'I had so-many points, so I had to bid such-and-such' is beyond hope.

Having made this point, I won't return to it again and will dispense with qualifying phrases such as 'provided the hand does not contain a singleton honour', 'so long as the playing strength is adequate', and so forth.

To return, the standard for an opening 1♣ is 16 points. The test is mainly one of high cards rather than playing strength, as these examples will make clear:

(1) ♠ K 9 4
♡ A 10 7 3
♢ Q J 2
♣ A Q 4

A flat enough hand, but a genuine 16 points and a sound 1♣ opening. Over any response at the one level you will rebid 1NT, which indicates 16–18.

(2) ♠ 5
♡ A K 10 9 7 4
♢ K Q J 8 6
♣ 4

Clearly a powerful hand, which you would much prefer to pick up than the one above. However, it might prove a mistake to open 1♣, as by the time you had shown your two suits and partner had added his high cards to yours, you might find you were too high. You present the best picture by opening 1♡ and taking vigorous action thereafter. (When I was writing a version of the Italian *Blue Club* for English readers I noted an observation by the Italian authors which is well worth bearing in mind: it is much easier, as the bidding develops, to *add* to the values you have shown than to *subtract* from them.)

It is quite right to open 1♣ on an exceptional hand such as:

(3) ♠ A Q J 10 8 5 2
♡ —
♢ A K 8 4
♣ 6 2

Here you have three first-round controls and will not be carried into space by a partner who may also have a good hand.

We will be considering the responses to 1♣, and the later sequences, in some detail, but first it may be helpful to examine the general scheme of responses.

Summary of responses to 1♣

Responding hands may be divided into general classes, as follows:

(a) Weak	First response
0–7	1♢ (negative)

(b) Limited with long suit

6-card major, 3–6	2♡ 2♠ (semi-positive)
7-card major, 4–6	3♡ 3♠
7-card minor, headed by	
A Q or K Q	3♣ 3♢

(c) Balanced types

8–10, no 5-card suit	1NT (positive)
11–13 or 16 upwards	2NT
14–15	3NT

(d) Fair values and fair suit

8 upwards, at least 5-card	
suit	1♡ 1♠ 2♣ 2♢ (positive)

(e) Fair 3-suiter

4–4–4–1, 8 upwards	1♢ (impossible negative)

It will be observed that 1♢ serves for two types of hand: normally a weak hand, but also a 4–4–4–1 type with positive values. The first impression is corrected on the next round and the sequence is known as the 'impossible negative'.

5

3 SEQUENCES FOLLOWING 1♣ AND THE NEGATIVE 1♦

The responder to 1♣ bids 1♦ on all weak hands in the 0–7 range, except for hands containing a long suit which qualify for the semipositive responses described in the next chapter. The developments following 1♣–1♦ are described under the following headings:

(a) Rebid on balanced hands.
(b) Rebid of 1♡ or 1♠.
(c) Rebid of 2♣ or 2♦.
(d) Rebid of 2♡ 2♠ 3♣ or 3♦.
(e) Rebid of 3♡ or 3♠.

(a) Rebid on balanced hands

Opener who is 4–4–3–2 or 4–3–3–3, or who is treating 5–3–3–2 as balanced, rebids 1NT on 16–18, 2NT on 19–21, 3NT on 24–26. (The 'gap' arises from the fact that 22–23 is represented by an opening 2NT.)

Sequences after 1♣–1♦–1NT (16–18)

It is convenient, for the most part, to adopt the same style of responses as over the opening 1NT of 13–15. As we shall see later, the general scheme for responder is as follows:

2♣   This is non-forcing Stayman, used either in search of a fit or when responder wants to make a mild game invitation. In the present context (where opener is marked with 16–18) responder, to invite game in a major, is likely to hold 6–7 points and perhaps 5–4–3–1 distribution. Thus 2♣ is the appropriate response on either of these hands:

	(1)	♠ J742	(2)	♠ KJ863
		♡ 9653		♡ 5
		◇ A752		◇ Q1062
		♣ 4		♣ 974

On (1) the responder looks for a better spot than 1NT and will pass any rebid. On (2) he intends to bid 2♠ over 2◇ or 2♡, indicating game possibilities. A jump to 3♠ at this point would be a still stronger invitation.

2◇   This is forcing Stayman. Opener rebids 2♡ or 2♠ with four, and otherwise bids 2NT. All continuations are game-forcing.

2♡ 2♠   Weak responses, which opener must pass.

2NT   Natural, a balanced 7 or 6 with a 5-card suit.   *←Minor*

3♣   3◇
3♡   3♠   These are special sequences, quite different in meaning from the same bids over an opening 1NT. They show the 'impossible negative' type— 4-4-4-1 with positive values (8 points upwards). The suit named is always the one below the singleton, 3♠ indicating that the singleton is in clubs. For a further account of this sequence, see Chapter 7:

3NT   Rare but natural, suggesting a maximum 1◇, probably 7 points and a 5-card minor.

4♣ 4◇   Transfers to 4♡ and 4♠ respectively. Respond 4◇ on:

> ♠ Q87632
> ♡ 104
> ◇ A982
> ♣ 7

The advantage of the transfer bid is (a) that the big hand is concealed, and (b) that the lead will come up to the big hand.

7

Sequences after 1♣–1♢–2NT (19–21)

Let it be said, first, that a rebid of 2NT on a flat 19 is unattractive. It is advisable to seek an alternative.

(1) ♠ K J 2   (2) ♠ A 4
       ♡ Q 7 3   ♡ K Q 6 3
       ♢ A K 4   ♢ A Q J
       ♣ A Q 6 2   ♣ K 8 5 3

On (1) rebid 1NT rather than 2NT. On (2) rebid 1♡.

When opener rebids 2NT responder acts as follows:

3♣   This is the Baron convention, asking for 4-card suits 'upwards' until a fit has been found or 3NT has been reached. When the opener's only 4-card (or 5-card) suit is clubs he rebids 3NT.

3♢   This is the Flint convention, used when responder proposes to subside in a major suit at the Three level. Say that he holds:

♠ 1 0 8 7 5 3 2
♡ 4
♢ J 7 3
♣ 9 4 2

Over 2NT he bids 3♢, which requires the opener to rebid 3♡. Now he transfers to 3♠, signifying that this is as high as he wants to go. When the opener is exceptionally strong in support of hearts he may spurn the transfer by rebidding 3♠ instead of 3♡. The partnership will then play in 3♠, if that is partner's suit, or in 4♡. When the opener is prepared to play in game whichever suit responder holds, he bids 4♡. When his main strength is in a minor suit he may bid 3NT over 3♢.

3♡ 3♠   Forcing, as in all systems. The sequence 2NT–3♡–3NT–4♡ carries a slam suggestion, as with determination to play in hearts and no slam interest responder would bid 4♡ directly over 2NT.

4♣ 4◇   Transfers to 4♡ and 4♠ respectively, as after 1♣–1◇–1NT.

Minor suit hands. On the rare occasions when the responder to 2NT has his values in a minor suit, or in both minors, and wants to go beyond 3NT, he must begin with 3♣ or 3◇. Thus 3◇ over 2NT is initially Flint, but when responder continues on the next round with 4♣ or 4◇ he presents a different picture.

Sequences after 1♣–1◇–3NT (24–26)

Now 4♣ is Baron, 4◇ weak transfer (like 3◇ over 2NT), 4♡ and 4♠ are constructive and forcing as far as 4NT.

(b) Rebid of 1♥ or 1♠

After 1♣–1◇ a rebid of 1♡ or 1♠ is not forcing and does not necessarily show a 5-card suit. On most hands where the opener holds four of a major, five of a minor, he rebids in the major suit. Thus with

$$♠ A Q 7 4$$
$$♡ 6$$
$$◇ A K J 7 3$$
$$♣ K 8 2$$

opener rebids 1♠ rather than 2◇. The main reason for this is that 1♠ allows responder to bid 1NT on very modest values and the opener can then introduce his second suit at a low level. Also, there is no risk of the partnership missing a good fit in a major suit.

The bidding after 1♣–1◇–1♡ (or 1♠) is one of the most important areas in the system. Before considering certain points of theory we will look at the general picture.

9

Responder's action after 1♣–1◇–1♡ (or 1♣–1◇–1♠)

Pass	Correct on any bad hand or on a flat 4 points, such as:

The Italians recom. a bid on a "good" Queen or more.

♠ Q 3 2
♡ 6 5 4
◇ 8 6 4 3
♣ Q 8 5

bid 2S if opener bid 1S

1♠	Biddable suit, 4–7 points, forcing for one round.
1NT	5–7 points, or 4 points when there is a prospect of finding a better fit.
2♣ 2◇	5-card suit, usually 5–7 points, constructive but not forcing.
2♡	Corresponds to a dead minimum (or sub-minimum) raise in a standard system, e.g.

♠ 10 8		♠ J 6 4
♡ Q 7 6 2	or	♡ K 8 2
◇ J 4 3		◇ 6 3
♣ 10 7 5 2		♣ 8 6 4 3 2

2

3♠ 3♣ 3◇	These jumps in a new suit denote precisely A Q x x x x or K Q x x x x, with at most a jack outside.

Nonsense!

In previous accounts of the system the jump at this point was used to signify an impossible negative type; a more economical scheme is proposed in Chapter 7.

If you had such a suit you would bid 2N in response to the 1C opening

2NT	This 'illogical' jump (as it is not consistent with a first-round negative) indicates an impossible negative type. See Chapter 7.
3♡	Corresponds to an average raise to two in a standard system, e.g.

> ♠ 6
> ♡ K 9 6 3
> ◇ J 7 6 4 3
> ♣ J 9 6

3♠ 4♣ 4◇   The double jump in a new suit indicates the values for a raise to four including a shortage in the suit named. Bid 4◇ on:

> ♠ A J 4
> ♡ Q 10 6 3
> ◇ 2
> ♣ 9 7 5 3 2

3NT   Values for a raise to four with particularly good trumps, e.g.

> ♠ 6 4
> ♡ K J 7 4 2
> ◇ K 8 5 3
> ♣ 6 3

4♡   Distributional raise with few high cards, e.g.

> ♠ 5
> ♡ Q 8 6 4 2
> ◇ 7
> ♣ 10 8 7 5 3 2

As this schedule makes clear, most developments in the lower ranges are natural and correspond to sequences over a normal 1♡ or 1♠ opening; that is to say, 1NT is the weakest response, a response at the two level shows fair values, and so forth. In the higher ranges all idle bids are put to effective use and are not difficult to remember. All bids that take the bidding beyond the three level must be based on trump support, so it is natural that double jumps should portray a side feature, in this case a singleton or void.

It is necessary to take a standpoint about the response of 1NT on minimum hands. In Goren's book on the system the implication is that with poor support for partner's suit and less than 5 points the responder should pass, whereas with 3-card support he should be more disposed to keep the bidding open with 1NT. I incline rather to the Blue Club theory (the Blue Club is an Italian system) that 1NT should, at first, have the character of a denial bid. Otherwise one of the main advantages of a one club system is lost – the advantage that the opener with a 2-suiter can generally rely on a chance to show both suits. This hand is a typical example:

West	East
♠ A K 7 4 2	♠ 5
♡ A Q 9 4 3	♡ K 8 5 2
♢ A 5	♢ 9 6 4 2
♧ 2	♧ J 7 5 4

West has a promising hand but his suits are not robust enough for an opening two bid. In a standard system the bidding is all too likely to languish in 1♠. Playing Precision, West opens 1♧ and the bidding continues:

West	East
1♧	1♢
1♠ (1)	1NT (2)
2♡	3♡
4♡	pass

(1) Having already shown a good hand, West is not under any pressure to jump at this point.

(2) As he has already limited his hand, East should not be afraid to try and improve the contract.

The play

Suppose a diamond is led against 4♡. The best technique for declarer is to win with the ace, cash the ace of spades and ruff a spade with a low trump. Then he plays a club to establish communications between the two hands.

The opponents will probably continue diamonds. West ruffs the third round and leads another low spade, ruffing with the eight. If, at worst, the spades are 5–2 and South overruffs, declarer retains the possibility of ruffing the other spade loser with the king of hearts. The contract will fail only against very hostile distribution.

The responder has to take a similar sort of decision – whether to pass or seek to improve the contract – when he holds a long minor suit and generally poor values. The bidding begins 1♣–1♢–1♠ and responder holds:

> ♠ 7
> ♡ 8 5
> ♢ Q J 9 7 5 4 2
> ♣ 10 6 4

He should risk a bid of 2♢. This is not forcing and proclaims a fair suit, though usually more than 3 points. If opener rebids 2♠ responder must give up, but over 2♡ or 2NT he can press on with 3♢, which must show this type of hand.

The principle that emerges from these two examples is that a Precision player should attempt to find a better strain even when the pursuit entails some risk.

In most cases an advance to the two level after opener has rebid 1♡ or 1♠ is based on fair values, more like the East hand in this example:

West	East
♠ A Q J 5 2	♠ 8 4
♡ A 10 5	♡ J 7 3
♢ J 7 4	♢ K Q 10 8 3
♣ A Q	♣ 9 5 2

This is another hand where players of a standard system would probably get off on the wrong foot, as East's response to 1♠ would be 1NT, placing the declaration in the wrong hand. At Precision the bidding goes:

West	East
1♣	1♢
1♠	2♢
2NT	3NT
pass	

With a minimum opening West would pass 2♢, but with 18 points and all suits guarded he is entitled to try for game.

The play

North leads the six of clubs against 3NT, South plays the jack and West the queen. A low diamond to the queen is allowed to win. As declarer will need a second trick from spades even if the diamonds can be brought in, he finesses the queen of spades while in dummy. When this holds he leads the jack of diamonds and overtakes. If the ace has still not appeared he takes another finesse in spades. The advantage of these manoeuvres appears when the ace of diamonds is held up and South holds K 10 x x in spades. With the aid of two finesses West can arrive at four spade tricks, one heart, two diamonds and two clubs.

(c) Rebid of 2♣ or 2♦

As we noted above, opener with a 4-card major and a 5-card minor tends to rebid in the major over a response of 1◊. As a player with a 5-card minor and 5–3–3–2 shape will usually rebid in notrumps, 2♣ and 2◊ more often than not reflect a 6-card suit. The exceptions occur when the major suit is too weak to mention or when only the minor suits are held, as in these examples:

(1)	♠ A K 8	(2)	♠ 6
	♡ J 6 4 3		♡ A Q 10
	◊ A K Q 8 5		◊ A K 8 6
	♣ 4		♣ A J 9 5 2

The rebid in a minor is neither weaker nor stronger than the rebid in a major, but there is an important difference in the style of responses. Since a strong hand containing a minor suit generally has an interest in 3NT, responses in a new suit at the two level are treated initially as 'notrump probes' and are forcing for one round, though they may not be at all strong. Some examples appear at the end of the schedule below.

Responder's action after 1♣–1◊–2◊ (or 1♣–1◊–2♣)

Pass	Up to 4 points, no suit worth showing, no support.
2♡ 2♠	May be a genuine suit, may be a notrump probe. Forcing for one round.
2NT	5–7 points with scattered values. Forcing in effect, as opener will always be able to rebid a 6-card suit or introduce a second suit.

14

3♣	Values concentrated in clubs, forcing for one round.
3♦	This single raise is the only limited, non-forcing response. It may be very weak, such as Q x x and a doubleton. With better values responder should bid some other suit to keep things going.
3♡ 3♠	These jumps indicate precisely A Q x x x x or K Q x x x x. They are analogous to the jump in a new suit after opener has rebid 1♡ or 1♠.
3NT	This would be 'impossible negative' with the singleton in partner's suit. See Chapter 7.

Mad.

A new suit at the two level, as explained above, may be a genuine suit, may be a notrump probe on a holding such as K x x x or even a 3-card suit such as A J x. These two examples will show how the response is handled:

West	East
♠ 10 4	♠ A Q 2
♡ A K 10	♡ 7 4 3
♦ A K J 9 7 5	♦ 6 4
♣ Q 4	♣ J 6 5 3 2

After 1♣–1♦–2♦ East bids 2♠, a notrump probe. This encourages West to bid 2NT and East is able to raise.

In the next example East again makes a notrump probe and West has support for the non-existent suit.

West	East
♠ A K 4	♠ 8 6 3 2
♡ A 8 2	♡ K Q 7
♦ 6	♦ 7 5 4 2
♣ A K 9 7 5 2	♣ J 6

This is a tricky hand for any sytem. At Precision the bidding might go:

West	East
1♣	1♦
2♣	2♡ (1)
2♠ (2)	3♣ (3)
3♡ (4)	3♠
4♣	pass

(1) East chooses the suit where he has a sure guard for no-trump purposes.

(2) West is not debarred from raising the hearts immediately, but 2♠ is more economical.

(3) East treats 2♠ for the moment as a further notrump probe. Having no stopper in diamonds he signs off in 3♣.

(4) West must not conceal his support for hearts, as East might hold a genuine suit.

Four clubs depends on not losing more than one trick in trumps. Players of a standard system might play in 1♣ if East displayed caution; but once East makes any response it is difficult to stop in any makable contract.

(d) Rebid of 2♥ 2♠ 3♣ 3♦

These jump rebids after 1♣–1♦ are forcing. Responder is in much the same situation as in a standard system after the bidding has begun 2♣–2♦. He must show where his values lie or, at worst, bid notrumps. The sequence is forcing as far as three of a suit that is not a new suit. Thus 1♣–1♦–2♥–2NT–3♥ can be passed by responder, and 1♣–1♦–2♣–2NT–3♣–3♠ can be passed by an opener who has lost heart.

Opener makes the forcing rebid on any hand that in the Acol system would be worth an opening 2♣ or an Acol two bid. The standard is at least as high because, remember, a rebid at the one level will evoke a response on quite slender values. One example will suffice:

	West		East
♠	A K J 8 7 5 3	♠	6 4 2
♥	A	♥	J 7 3
♦	K 7 2	♦	A J 5 4
♣	A Q	♣	8 6 5

The bidding goes:

West		East	
1♣		1♦	
2♣		3♦	(1)
4♦	(2)	4♠	
5♣	(3)	5♦	
5♥		5♠	
6♠	(4)	pass	

16

(1) With a weaker hand East would bid 2NT or, perhaps, 3♣. He is good enough to show the diamonds *en route*.

(2) 3♠ at this point would no doubt be forcing, but the diamond support might be of more interest to the weaker hand.

(3) It is possible for partner to hold ◇ A Q x x x and three low spades, so West explores the possibility of a grand slam by starting a chain of cue bids.

(4) By this time it is apparent that East has not all the cards required for seven.

The play

North leads a heart against 6♠. If all follow to the ace of spades West draws the outstanding trump and follows with ace, king and a third diamond towards the J x. Whenever diamonds are 3-3, or North has the queen, or South has Q x, the contract will be safe without the club finesse.

(e) Rebid of 3♥ or 3♠

This double jump after 1♣–1◇ is available on the very rare hands where <u>opener wishes to set the suit and inquire immediately for controls</u>. Responder's first duty is to name an ace or bid 3NT. Opener may then inquire for kings (or a singleton with sufficient trump support) by making a relay bid in the next suit. It works like this:

	West	East
♠	A K Q 10 8 7 4	9 6 5
♥	A K Q 9	10 5 2
◇	—	Q 8 7 6 4 2
♣	Q 5	8

The bidding goes:

West	East
1♣	1◇
3♠	3 NT(1)
4♣ (2)	5♣ (3)
6♠ (4)	pass

17

(1) No ace.

(2) Asking for kings. The inquiry is safe because if partner shows the (unwanted) king of diamonds West can close shop in 4♠.

(3) 'You asked me, and a singleton with three trumps ought to be as good as a king.'

(4) 'Yes, thank you!'

The play

North leads a diamond against 6♠. West may want to ruff twice, so he leads the queen of clubs at trick 2. The defenders win and play a trump, to which all follow. After ruffing the club West should not draw the outstanding trump but should play off two top hearts and, if the jack does not fall, a third heart. This gains when the same defender holds J x x x of hearts and two trumps, as declarer will then be able to ruff the fourth round of hearts with impunity.

Summary

The summaries at the end of most chapters will, I hope, be useful as an aid to memory.

(a) **After 1♣–1♦–1NT (16–18)** 2♣ is non-forcing Stayman, any continuation in a major is invitational; 2♦ is forcing Stayman, 2♥ 2♠ weak; responses at the three level are impossible negative, the suit named being the one below the singleton; 4♣ and 4♦ are transfers to 4♥ and 4♠ respectively.

After 1♣–1♦–2NT (19–21) 3♣ is Baron, 3♦ Flint, 4♣ and 4♦ are transfers.

After 1♣–1♦–3NT (24–26) 4♣ is Baron, 4♦ Flint, 4♥ and 4♠ are forcing to 4NT.

(b) **After 1♣–1♦–1♥ (or 1♠)** 1NT is 4–7; 2♣ 2♦ fair suit; jump in new suit six to A Q or K Q; 2NT impossible negative; double jump values for game raise, shortage in the suit named; 3NT raise to game with good trumps; raise to 4♥ distributional.

(c) **After 1♣–1♦–2♣ (or 2♦)** new suit at two level may be

notrump probe; jump new suit six to A Q or K Q; 3NT impossible negative.

(d) 1♣–1◊–2♥ etc. is forcing to the three level.

(e) 1♣–1◊–3♥ (or 3♠) sets the suit and asks for aces, subsequent relay asks for lowest second-round control.

4 SEMI-POSITIVE RESPONSES TO 1♣

The semi-positive responses to 1♣ express very accurately hands with a long suit that do not qualify for a positive (normally 8 points upwards). There are three types:

(a) 2♥ and 2♠, 6-card major, 3–6 points.
(b) 3♥ and 3♠, 7-card major, 4–6 points.
(c) 3♣ and 3◊, 7-card minor headed by A Q or K Q.

(a) The response of 2♥ or 2♠

These responses give an immediate picture of a hand containing a 6-card major with 4–6 points, or possibly a 7-card suit with only 3 points. Ideally, the strength should be concentrated in the suit. These are good examples:

(1)	♠ 5	(2)	♠ Q 10 8 7 6 4 2
	♥ K Q 10 8 6 3		♥ 5 3
	◊ 7 4 2		◊ J 6 2
	♣ 10 7 3		♣ 4

see note page 10

It is a mistake to respond 2♥ or 2♠ on a hand that is potentially useful in some other strain. These two hands are *not* suitable:

(3)	♠ 5	(4)	♠ A Q 8 6 4 2
	♥ J 9 7 6 4 2		♥ 4
	◊ 8 3		◊ 10 7 6 5 3
	♣ A J 8 5		♣ 6

Hand (3) has too little in hearts and too much outside. Hand (4) could be a powerful hand in either spades or diamonds and for that reason does not qualify for a response that is strictly limited.
The range is 3–6 rather than 3–7 because a 7-point hand with a good 6-card major qualifies for a positive response of 1♥ or 1♠.

Opener's rebid after 1♣–2♡ (or 1♣–2♠)

Pass
: Whenever game seems unlikely after this precise response.

New suit
: Forcing for one round, invites support on x x x or Q x. Responder's weakest rebid is a repeat of his own suit.

2NT
: Forcing, provisionally confirms hearts. Responder who is better than minimum should either show a feature in a side suit or, with a suit headed by A Q or K Q, bid 3NT. After 1♣–2♡–2NT responder holds:

> (1) ♠ 5
> ♡ K J 8 6 3 2
> ♢ Q 10 8
> ♣ 9 5 2

As he is not minimum he bids 3♢, showing a side feature:

> (2) ♠ 9 5
> ♡ Q J 9 7 5 3
> ♢ J 4 2
> ♣ 6 3

Holding a minimum, he rebids 3♡.

> (3) ♠ 8 4 2
> ♡ A Q 8 6 4 3
> ♢ 7 4 3
> ♣ 6

To show a suit headed by A Q or K Q he bids 3NT.

3♡
: A natural try for game in the suit. Responder may pass with a minimum.

3NT
: To play, warns partner not to persist with his suit.

Perhaps the most useful function of the semi-positive is that it enables the partnership to stop at a low level when opener can judge early on that game prospects are not good.

West	East
♠ 4	♠ K J 10 7 5 3
♥ A K 9 5 4	♥ 6 2
♦ A J 4	♦ 7 5 3
♣ K Q 10 9	♣ 5 4

Players using standard methods would probably go overboard on this hand. The bidding would begin 1♥–1♠, 2♣–2♠, and West would be tempted to make one more try with 2NT. The Precision bidding is 1♣–2♠ – finish!

The play

The best way to play the trumps in a spade contract is low to the king and, if this holds, low on the next round. This keeps the losers to two when the suit divides 3–3 and also when South has Q x.

(b) The response of 3♥ or 3♠

These responses indicate a hand on which the player would have opened with a pre-emptive three bid as dealer, not vulnerable. This would be a typical hand:

♠ K Q 10 8 6 5 3
♥ 5 4
♦ 6 4 2
♣ 4

It should not be difficult for the opener to judge his rebid in this very familiar situation.

With an 8-card suit (but still not more than 6 points) responder might bid four of his suit over 1♣.

(c) The response of 3♣ or 3♦

There would be little point in making these jumps on a weak hand. They are used instead to display a suit of precisely A Q x x x x or K Q x x x x, information that can be of great help to the opener.

22

	West		East
♠	A K Q 6 3	♠	7 4
♡	A Q 8 5	♡	6 2
◊	K 8	◊	10 4
♣	K 5	♣	A Q 9 7 6 4 2

After 1♣–3♣ West can count eleven likely tricks at notrumps, with the certainty of a twelfth if the opening lead is a heart or a diamond. Playing for a top, he goes direct to 6NT.

The play

If North is inconsiderate enough to lead a black suit, West should play off the top spades to clarify the situation in that suit. If this brings no joy he must run down the clubs and judge from the discards whether to take a heart finesse for the twelfth trick, or to lead up to the king of diamonds, or to attempt a throw-in which would succeed if North held both key cards, the king of hearts and the ace of diamonds. The simple heart finesse is likely to be the best chance because North's failure to lead a diamond after this bidding makes it slightly more likely than otherwise that he holds the ace. Holding the ace, he would not lead it; not holding this card, he might have done so.

Summary

(a) The response of 2♡ or 2♠ to 1♣ suggests a 6-card suit with 4–6 points or possibly a 7-card suit with only 3 points. A rebid of 2NT by opener is forcing. Responder with better than a minimum shows a side feature; with a suit headed by A Q or K Q he bids 3NT.

(b) The responses of 3♡ or 3♠ show a hand equal to an opening three bid, namely a 7-card suit and about 4–6 points.

(c) The responses of 3♣ or 3◊ denote a 7-card suit headed by A Q or K Q.

5 NOTRUMP RESPONSES TO 1♣

We move now to the area of positive responses to 1♣. As a positive response in a suit promises five cards, a responder who has 8 points and 4-3-3-3 or 4-4-3-2 distribution must respond in notrumps. These are the requirements:

    (a)   Response of 1NT, 8-10.
    (b)   Response of 2NT, 11-13 or 16 upwards.
    (c)   Response of 3NT, 14-15.

(a) Response of 1NT, 8-10

The opener's rebids over the response of 1NT are mostly natural, as will appear from the following schedule.

Opener's rebid after 1♣–1NT

2♣	This is Stayman, asking responder to name a 4-card major or bid 2◇.
2◇ 2♡ 2♠	All natural, at least a 5-card suit, and in effect forcing to game.
2NT	Minimum balanced opening, not forcing.

It is possible to devise meanings for a jump to three of a suit, or to treat 3♣ as some form of conventional inquiry, but the advantage is too slight for it to be worth while.

Whenever there is a positive response to 1NT the partners know they have a minimum of 24 between them. However, 24 points will not usually be enough for game when there is no 5-card suit around, so there is provision, after 1♣–1NT, for the bidding to stop in 2NT. There are just two non-forcing sequences, one of which we have already listed:

	(1)	West	East	(2)	West	East
		1♣	1NT		1♣	1NT
		2NT	pass		2♣	2 any
					2NT	pass

Here is an example of the second sequence:

West	East
♠ 652	♠ AK73
♡ K72	♡ A10
◇ KQ53	◇ 9642
♣ 1065	♣ AJ3

With East the dealer, the bidding goes:

West	East
—	1♣
1NT	2♣
2◇	2NT
pass	

After his Stayman inquiry has borne no fruit East indicates a minimum 16 by bidding 2NT. West, also with a minimum with sterile 4–3–3–3 shape, has no reason to go further.

The play

North opens a low heart against 2NT and dummy's ten holds the trick. After this fortunate beginning West needs only two tricks from diamonds and can afford one of the game's lesser known safety plays: he ducks the first round of diamonds in both hands, a play that saves the vital trick when North has a singleton ace. Whatever happens on the first diamond West will always be able to develop two tricks when the suit is breaking 3–2 or when South holds A 10 x x.

It is advisable, on balance, to treat the following sequence as forcing:

	West	East
(3)	1♣	1NT
	2♣	2♡
	3♡	

Holding a minimum of 24 points and a fit in a major suit, the partners do not want to languish at the three level. The advantage of the raise to three being forcing is that when West is better than minimum, but not sure whether he wants to play in hearts or notrumps, he is not obliged to take a stab at one or the other. Also, West may be strong and want to set the suit before cue-bidding.

When the opener rebids 2♦ 2♥ or 2♠, showing a minimum of five cards, all sequences are game-forcing.

West	East
♠ A 9 3	♠ K Q 5
♥ 7 4	♥ A K J 8 3
♦ J 9 6 4	♦ K 10
♣ A 10 7 2	♣ K 5 3

With East speaking first, the bidding goes:

West	East
—	1♣
1NT	2♥
2NT	3NT
pass	

West is confident of game but does not jump over 2♥ because his partner is unlimited and may be intending to introduce another suit.

The play

North leads the jack of spades against 3NT. To make sure of the contract, West should win with the king and lead the king of diamonds from the table. This way, he can be sure of two diamond tricks, with seven top winners in the other suits.

(b) Response of 2NT, 11–13 or 16 upwards

A response of 2NT suggests, initially, 11–13 with no 5-card suit and no singleton. The only conventional rebid by the opener is 3♣, which is best played as Baron, asking for 4-card suits upwards. It is otherwise difficult sometimes to arrive at minor-suit slams.

West	East
♠ A 5 4	♠ K 6
♥ A K 7 3	♥ Q 9 2
♦ Q 6	♦ K 9 5 2
♣ A Q 10 4	♣ K J 8 7

The bidding goes:

West	East
1♣	2NT
3♣ (1)	3◇
3♡	3NT (2)
4♣ (3)	5♣
6♣	pass

(1) Baron, asking for 4-card suits 'upwards'.

(2) The Baron sequence normally ends at 3NT. East is not denying four clubs, he simply indicates that he has no other 4-card suit to show below 3NT.

(3) However, West is strong enough to make one more try. If partner cannot raise the clubs the hand can be played in 4♡ or 4NT.

The play

Knowing that the cunning Precisioneers have arrived in a 4–4 fit, North will probably open a trump against 6♣. If dummy's seven is covered by the nine, West wins and leads the queen of diamonds from hand. Say that the opponents take the second diamond and lead another trump. Declarer can now play on reverse dummy lines, ruffing two diamonds and drawing the trumps with dummy's K J.

The responder to 1♣ will seldom hold a balanced (or unbalanced) 16 points, but when he does there is no need for a mighty leap. He bids 2NT and if partner bids 3NT he comes again with 4♣, Baron. With a minimum of 32 points he can afford to take the bidding to 4NT, at the very least.

(c) Response of 3NT, 14–15

3NT is not the easiest of responses to manage and throughout the system it is assigned the narrow range of 14–15. When the opener wants to explore further he bids 4♣, Baron. All

continuations are forcing as far as 4NT. Here is an example of a
hand where the problem is to stop in time:

West	East
♠ K 8 4	♠ A Q 7 3
♡ A Q 5	♡ K J 4
◇ Q J 3	◇ A 8 5 2
♣ Q 10 6 2	♣ A 7

In a pairs contest half the field would arrive at an impossible
slam through lack of machinery to establish in time that the hands
did not fit well. At Precision the bidding goes:

West	East
—	1♣
3NT	4♣ (1)
4NT	pass (2)

(1) With 18 points opposite his partner's minimum of 14, East
looks for a 4–4 fit.

(2) As his partner has by-passed the other suits he must hold
four clubs and his distribution must be precisely 3-3-3-4. That is
the worst news that East could hear, so prudently he passes.

The play

North leads the ten of hearts against 4NT. Declarer wins in
dummy with the jack and leads a diamond to the queen and king.
North plays a second heart, taken by the ace.

West plays off two rounds of diamonds and three rounds of
spades. If nothing breaks, even 4NT become perilous. The best
continuation may be to cash the king of hearts and exit in the suit
of which South holds four. South will then have to open up the
clubs, giving declarer additional chances.

Summary

(a) **After the response of 1NT (8–10)** 2♣ is Stayman,
2◇ 2♡ 2♠ denote a 5-card suit and are forcing to game. The
bidding may stop in 2NT after 1♣–1NT–2NT or after a Stayman
inquiry has failed to discover a 4–4 fit in a major. When responder

shows a major over 2♣, as in the sequence 1♣–1NT–2♣–2♠, a raise to three is forcing.

(b) **After the response of 2NT (11–13 or 16 upwards)** 3♣ is Baron. When responder holds 16 or more he first bids 2NT and, over a rebid of 3NT, comes again with 4♣, Baron.

(c) **After the response of 3NT (14–15)** 4♣ is Baron, forcing to 4NT.

6 POSITIVE RESPONSES TO 1♣

When the responder to 1♣ holds upwards of 8 points and has a 5-card suit, he bids the suit at minimum level. The sequence is forcing to 2NT and can stop there, or at the three level, only when there is positive evidence of a misfit. Thus 1♣–1♥–1NT–2NT is forcing and either player might have plenty in reserve; but 1♣–1♥–1♠–2♥–2♠–2NT, where it looks as though each player is short in his partner's long suit, could be dropped.

We consider positive responses, and the problems arising, under the following headings:

    (a) Responding 1♥ or 1♠.
    (b) Responding 2♣ or 2♦.
    (c) The problem of strong responding hands.
    (d) What about asking bids?
    (e) Sequences after a raise of a positive response.

(a) Responding 1♥ or 1♠

While the normal standard is 8 points, responder may give a positive when he holds a 6-card major and 7 points, as in the West hand below:

	West	East
♠	4	A J 6
♥	K J 9 7 6 2	A 5 3
♦	Q 10 3	A K 6 4
♣	J 8 6	Q 7 3

One advantage of allowing a response of 1♥ on West's hand is that this narrows the range of the semi-positive jump to 2♥. Apart from that, West may have a problem if he begins with a negative 1♦. Suppose East's rebid is 1♠: then it is dangerous to bid only 2♥, which is not forcing, and there is no good alternative. Thus on the present hand the bidding would go:

West	East
—	1♣
1♡	1NT (1)
2♡	3♡ (2)
4♡	pass

(1) Following a sound general principle, East makes the same rebid as he would have done over a negative 1◇.

(2) East has ample for game, but once a fit has been established the bidding cannot die. It is normal to proceed slowly, in case partner is strong and intends to cue-bid. *(Sean !)*

The play   *Principle of Fast Arrival*

North leads a spade against 4♡. Declarer's best line is to take the ace of spades and ruff a spade, cross to ace of hearts and ruff the last spade. Then he plays a diamond to the king and leads the three of hearts, putting in the jack if South follows with a low trump. If North is able to win, the best he can do is return a diamond into the Q 10. West cashes the two diamonds, leads the two of hearts to dummy's five, and discards a club on the ace of diamonds.

The Precision style is well adapted to hands where the combined values are in the game zone but there is no suit that can be readily established. Here is an awkward hand on which most players would get too high:

West	East
♠ A J 8 6 3	♠ Q 5
♡ K 10 7 4 2	♡ A 5
◇ 6	◇ A Q 9 7 5 2
♣ 9 4	♣ A 10 8

The bidding goes:

West	East
—	1♣
1♠	2◇
2♡	2NT (1)
3♡	3♠
pass (2)	

(1) 2♠ would not be a mistake at this point, but East has a fair guard in the unbid suit and there will probably be an opportunity to support spades later.

(2) West can see that the hands are not fitting well. His partner has made limited bids, so West is free to pass.

The play

3♠ is no sinecure but is better than playing in game. Against a club lead West should play on cross-ruff lines. He begins with ace of diamonds and a diamond ruff, two top hearts and a third heart, ruffed with the queen of spades if North follows suit. There is a good chance to scramble nine tricks.

(b) Responding 2♣ or 2♦

Positive responses in a minor suit carry the same message – 8 points and a 5-card suit. The requirements may be shaded when responder holds a suit of A K x x x x or a powerful minor 2-suiter such as:

> ♠ 3
> ♡ 4
> ◊ A 10 8 6 4 2
> ♣ K 9 7 6 3

If responder does not begin with a positive he will have a problem on the second round.

The bidding might end in four of a minor after a response of 2♣ or 2♦, but otherwise the sequence is forcing to game. There is not time to establish a *misfit* below the level of 3NT, and if a sequence such as 1♣–2◊–2♡–3◊–3♡ could be dropped at any point, players would not be able to develop their hands naturally.

There are no conventional sequences after the response in a minor suit and the bidding generally proceeds quite easily when the responder is in the lower range. Here is an example from tournament play where the partners were able to exchange all the important information:

32

	West		East
♠	A K 8 6 5 3	♠	J 7 4
♡	A 7 6 3	♡	Q 8
◇	K 4	◇	A Q 10 6 2
♣	A	♣	J 6 3

The bidding went:

West	East
1♣	2◇
2♠	3♠ (1)
4♣ (2)	4◇
4♡	4♠
5◇	6♠ (3)
pass	

(1) As the spades are surely a 5-card suit, J x x is sufficient for a raise; but 2NT at this point would not be a mistake.

(2) West begins a chain of cue-bidding, starting with his lowest ace.

(3) News that partner holds the king of diamonds transforms the East hand. Having signed off before, he can now accept the slam invitation.

The play

A heart lead against 6♠ was covered by the queen, king and ace. Two top trumps left North still in possession of the queen. After these unfavourable developments West had to play for a long shot. He finessed the ten of diamonds on the second round and disposed of all his heart losers in time, as North held J x x x of diamonds in addition to Q x x of trumps.

The difficult hands tend to be those where the responder to 1♣ holds the values for an opening bid, or more. That brings us to the next section.

(c) The problem of strong responding hands

West opens 1♣ and East holds a hand of this type:

$$♠ \ 842$$
$$♡ \ AQ963$$
$$♢ \ KJ4$$
$$♣ \ A7$$

He gives a positive of 1♡ and opener bids 2♣. For the moment responder bids 2♢, to carry things along. Now West bids 2NT. Where next? 3♣ presumably, but meanwhile East is not giving a good picture either of his distribution or his values. The problem can be still worse when the first response is at the two level. The responder makes artificial bids to keep the auction alive, but feels he is floating.

It is interesting to observe, in passing, that this is the most difficult area in standard systems also. Opener has between 15 and 18 points, responder between 13 and 16. Both players know that, with a good fit, there may be a slam, but it is often difficult to proceed.

Having stated the problem I must suggest a solution. Asking bids, which are discussed in the next paragraph, can be helpful on certain hands. Another possibility, which I put forward as a suggestion and not as an integral part of the system, is to make 1NT a two-way response. Initially, it shows the balanced 8–10; but when the responder follows up with a bid of a new suit at the three level he shows a hand in the 13–15 range, probably 5-3-3-2 or 5-4-2-2. Hands with more pronounced distribution are easier to manage in a natural way, and on hands of 16 or more it is safe to carry the bidding beyond 3NT, so long as one can always subside in 4NT. So suppose the bidding goes:

(1) 1♣   1NT   or   (2) 1♣   1NT
     2♡   3♣   2♣ (Stayman)   3♠

In each case responder's bid at the three level on the second round denotes the 5-3-3-2 type in the 13–15 range. This method is easy to play and works well; but it is optional and a matter for partnership agreement.

(d) What about asking bids ?

All previous accounts of Precision have featured the use of asking bids in a particular area. After a positive response a raise by the opener, in a sequence such as 1♣–1♡–2♡, is a trump asking bid, requesting the responder to define his trump holding. With no top honour (ace, king, or queen) he advances one step, 2♠; with a 5-card suit and one top honour, two steps, 2NT; and so it goes on. After a *trump asking bid* any new suit is a *control asking bid*, demanding specific information about partner's holding in this second suit. There are also *ace asking bids*, where a jump in a new suit after a positive response requests information about partner's holding in the new suit and about his side aces.

It is not difficult to provide pretty examples showing what these sequences can achieve, and some writers dwell in that garden for many pages. I feel, however, that these asking bids perch rather awkwardly on the system, like a bob on a woollen cap; that they operate in too limited an area; and that the Italian-style asking bids described in Chapter 19 are better devised.

(e) Sequences after a raise of a positive response

When formal asking bids are not being played it is advisable to have certain understandings about the sequences following a raise of a positive response. The bidding begins 1♣–1♠–2♠ and as responder you hold:

♠ J8642
♡ KJ3
♢ AK54
♣ 3

These are useful values opposite an opener who is more or less unlimited, but if you start to show your controls in the other suits you will be haunted throughout the auction by fears about your bad trumps. For that reason the next bid should be tied to your trump holding in the following way:

Responder's next bid after 1♣–1♡–2♡ (or 1♣–1♠–2♠)

3♡ Warns of bad trumps (Q x x x x at best).

3NT Shows upwards of K Q x x x in the trump suit with no side control (king or singleton). Bid 3NT on:

> ♠ Q 6
> ♡ A Q 10 6 4
> ◊ J 5 4 2
> ♣ 6 4

4♡ Shows upwards of K Q x x x x with no side control. Bid 4♡ on:

> ♠ 8 5
> ♡ K Q J 7 4 2
> ◊ Q 10 8
> ♣ 6 3

2NT Standard mark-time bid on hands with reasonable trumps (better than Q x x x x) and some outside feature. Bid 2NT on:

> ♠ J 7 2
> ♡ A 9 6 4 3
> ◊ K 6 5
> ♣ J 4

or

> ♠ 5
> ♡ K Q 8 6 4
> ◊ K Q 6 3 2
> ♣ 5 2

New suit Shows the *ace* of this suit and *very fair* trumps (K J x x x upwards). Bid 3◊ on:

> ♠ Q 7 6
> ♡ K J 10 8 5
> ◊ A 6 3
> ♣ 7 4

36

It will be noted that the space-consuming calls, 3NT and four of the suit, show hands of strictly limited strength, but with goodish trumps. This will put partner perfectly in the picture.

To revert to our original example, where as responder you held:

♠ J8642
♡ KJ3
◇ AK54
♣ 3

After 1♣–1♠–2♠ you bid 3♠, warning of bad trumps. If, despite this warning, partner makes some forward-going move, you are away!

After 1♣–2♣–3♣ (or 1♣–2◇–3◇) there is not space to follow the same schedule, but here again 4♣ would carry the meaning, 'Trump suit poor'.

Summary

(a) The response of 1♡ or 1♠ denotes upwards of 8 points and a 5-card suit, or sometimes 7 points and a 6-card suit. The bidding may stop in 2NT or at the three level only when there is evidence of a misfit.

(b) The response of 2♣ or 2◇ denotes 8 points and a 5-card suit, occasionally 7 points in a well distributed hand. It is forcing to game or to at least four of a minor.

(c) **Strong responding hands**, especially 5–3–3–2 and 5–4–2–2 types, are the most difficult to manage. The following suggestion is optional: with 13–15 and one of the above distributions, first respond 1NT and then bid the suit at the three level.

(d) **Asking bids** of various types can be made when there has been a positive response to 1♣. A scheme is described in chapter 19. Asking bids are optional.

(e) **After a raise of a positive response**, assuming that asking bids are not being played, responder rebids as follows: 3 of his suit with bad trumps (Qxxxx at best); 3NT with KQxxx or better in trumps and no side king or singleton; 4 of his suit with KQxxxx or better and no side control; 2NT with reasonable trumps and some outside feature; new suit to show the ace and very fair trumps (KJxxx upwards).

7 THE 'IMPOSSIBLE NEGATIVE' COMPLEX

Partner opens 1♣ and you hold:

> ♠ Q 10 7 4
> ♥ 6
> ♦ A J 8 4
> ♣ Q 9 5 3

Ample for a positive, but you have no 5-card suit and cannot reasonably bid 1NT with a singleton. What you do is respond 1♦ and subsequently take action inconsistent with the negative response, which is then seen to have been 'impossible'. Hence the term, 'impossible negative'.

In earlier versions of the system responder was exhorted to follow with a jump in notrumps when partner bid the singleton (in the present example, 1♣–1♦–1♥–2NT) and to jump in the suit of the singleton when partner rebid in notrumps or in any other suit (1♣–1♦–1NT-3♥ or 1♣–1♦–1♣–3♥).

These impossible negative sequences are quite rare, and I feel it is uneconomic to devote so many sequences to them. As the reader may recall, I suggested that the jump following a negative should indicate precise holdings (A Q x x x x or K Q x x x x) in the suit named. There are other ways of dealing with the 4-4-4-1 types. This is the scheme I propose:

(a) When opener rebids 1♥ or 1♠

After 1♣–1♦–1♥ (or 1♣–1♦–1♠) responder always jumps to 2NT. Opener rebids 3♣ (a relay) to discover where the singleton lies. With a singleton in hearts (the suit opened) responder bids 3♥ with 8–10 or 14 upwards, 3NT with 11–13. So you get these sequences:

	West	East
(1)	1♣	1♦
	1♥	2NT (impossible negative)
	3♣ (forced)	3♥ (singleton ♥)
	3NT	pass

Here it is plain that East has the lower range, 8–10.

(2)	1♣	1♢
	1♡	2NT (impossible negative)
	3♣ (forced)	3♡ (singleton ♡)
	3NT	4 any

When East advances over 3NT he indicates the higher range, 14 upwards.

(3)	1♣	1♢
	1♠	2NT (impossible negative)
	3♣ (forced)	3NT (singleton ♠)

This time East shows precisely 11–13 with a singleton of his partner's suit.

Suppose, next, that responder is 4-4-4-1 with **support** for his partner. Very simple: over 3♣ he indicates his singleton. The bidding progresses in this fashion:

(4)	1♣	1♢
	1♡	2NT
	3♣	4♣ (singleton ♣)
	4♡	?

(5)	1♣	1♢
	1♠	2NT
	3♣	3♡ (singleton ♡)
	4♢	?

In (4) West indicates a minimum 1♣ opening by declining to make any cue-bid when East shows his support. In (5) West co-operates by cue-bidding his lowest side ace. If East has nothing much in reserve he will bid 4♠ and leave the next move to his partner.

(b) When opener rebids 2♣ or 2♦

There is less room now to express the different ranges and the identity of the singleton, but the bidding is simplified by the fact that any response at the two level is temporarily forcing.

When responder's singleton is in the opener's suit and he is in the lower or medium range (8–11) he bids 3NT.

♠ K 8 6 3
♡ Q 9 5 4   After 1♣–1♢–2♢ bid 3NT.
♢ J
♣ K 10 8 6

When the singleton is in opener's suit and responder has 12 or more he bids 2NT for the moment and advances later. 2NT is forcing, remember. The bidding can always stop in 4NT.

♠ K J 8 6
♡ Q 10 4 2   After 1♣–1♢–2♣ bid 2NT and, if partner
♢ A Q J 3   rebids 3NT, advance to 4NT.
♣ 4

When the singleton is in a different suit, bid a suit at the two level (forcing) and take it from there.

♠ A Q 7 3
♡ J 8 4 2   After 1♣–1♢–2♣ bid 2♠ for the present
♢ 5   and if partner rebids, say, 2NT, jump to 4♣.
♣ K 7 4 3

(c) When opener rebids in notrumps

To show the impossible negative after 1♣–1♢–1NT, jump to the three level in the suit *below the singleton* – 3♠ when the singleton is in clubs. If the news does not excite the opener he rebids 3NT; if he is interested he makes an economical call in the next suit, the suit of the singleton.

	West		East
♠	A 8 5	♠	K J 6 4
♡	K 7	♡	A 8 5 2
♢	A 10 7 4	♢	6
♣	A Q 9 5	♣	K 8 4 3

The bidding goes:

West	East
1♣	1♢
1NT	3♣ (1)
3♢ (2)	3♡
4♣ (3)	4♠ (4)
5♢ (5)	6♣
pass	

(1) Indicates 4–4–1–4 with positive values. Responder bids the suit below the singleton, remember.

(2) West is 'interested' and signifies this by bidding the suit of the known singleton. (Had partner bid 3♠, showing a singleton club, West would have been less impressed and would have signed off in 3NT.)

(3) West discloses the suit in which he intends to play.

(4) Showing a further control, on the basis that clubs are the agreed suit.

(5) West's previous bid in diamonds meant simply that he was interested in a slam. Now he admits to holding the ace.

The play

A trump is the most awkward lead against 6♣ and we will say that North opens the two of clubs. The best line (in preference to trying to ruff three diamonds) is to go up with the king of clubs, lead a diamond to the ace and ruff a diamond, then return to the king of hearts and finesse the jack of spades. If this loses and the defenders play a second trump West will have various chances, either from a 3–3 spade break or a squeeze.

To return to the bidding: should the opener rebid 2NT over 1◇, a responder with the impossible negative type can set things in motion by bidding 3♣ (Baron).

Summary

A responder to 1♣ who holds 4–4–4–1 distribution and upwards of 8 points bids 1◇ for the moment. Then:

(a) **When opener rebids 1♡ or 1♠** he bids 2NT and opener must bid 3♣ (forced). Then responder with a singleton of opener's suit bids 3 of that suit with 8–10 or 14 upwards, bids 3NT with 11–13; with support for opener he bids the suit of his singleton.

(b) **When opener rebids 2♣ or 2◇** responder with a singleton of opener's suit and 8–11 bids 3NT; with 12 he bids 2NT and advances later; with support for opener and a singleton elsewhere he bids a new suit at the two level and takes it from there.

(c) When opener rebids 1NT responder bids the suit below his singleton at the three level (3♧ with a singleton in clubs). If opener is interested he makes a waiting bid in the suit of the known singleton.

8 WHEN THERE IS INTERVENTION OVER 1♣

There is a popular belief that one club systems can be thrown out of gear by intervention. 'Suppose that over 1♣ the next player can bid 2♠', the theory runs, 'then the players have to start exchanging information about their real suits at the three level.'

The main answer to that is that the assurance of a strong opening, 16 points or more, gives the side at least as good a basis for further action as a nebulous one bid in standard systems.

Intervention at a low level is by no means obstructive; properly countered, it adds to the number of calls available to the responder and enables him to tell more than he would have been able to do after a pass. The general strategy is to profit from this factor and to be deflected as little as possible from the normal processes of constructive bidding. Penalization of the opponents, who probably have some low plot, is not a primary objective. This is the recommended schedule:

(a) When second hand doubles 1♣

The double provides responder with two additional calls – pass and redouble. He acts as follows:

With 0–4, pass.
With 5–7 and no 4-card major, bid 1♢.
With 5–7 and at least one 4-card major, redouble.
With 4–6 and a 6-card major, bid a semi-positive 2♡ or 2♠.
With 8 or more, give a normal positive response.

South opens 1♣, West doubles, and North holds:

(1)   ♠ Q 10 8 7 4
      ♡ 5 2
      ♢ 7 3
      ♣ J 9 6 2

Holding fewer than 5 points, North must pass for the moment.

(2)   ♠ 7 4
      ♡ K 6 2
      ♢ Q 8 5
      ♣ J 8 7 6 2

Holding between 5 and 7 points but no 4-card major, he makes a free bid of 1◇. One advantage of the scheme is that the 1♣ opener, holding a 4-card major, is not obliged to bid it for the information of the enemy.

(3) ♠ J 4
       ♡ K 10 8 7 4
       ◇ 7 3
       ♣ Q 7 5 3

Holding a 4-card (or longer) major, but not enough for a positive, North redoubles.

(4) ♠ 10 8 6
       ♡ A J 8 3
       ◇ Q 8 6 4
       ♣ Q 5

With the values for a positive, bid 1NT. Don't waste time trying to penalize the opponents at a low level; they probably have a bolt-hole of some sort.

(5) ♠ Q 8 5 4
       ♡ 6
       ◇ K 10 8 6
       ♣ K 8 5 4

If you are going to be awkward and ask 'What do you do with an impossible negative type?' the answer is that there is no harm in redoubling with something in hand.

(b) When second hand overcalls at the one level

With 0–4, pass.

With 5–7, double. This, of course, is a 'negative' or 'sputnik' double, not for penalties.

With 8–10 and a guard in the opponent's suit, bid 1NT.

With upwards of 8 and a 5-card suit, make the normal positive response.

With upwards of 8 and no guard, either double with something in hand or, when not minimum, cue-bid the opponent's suit.

South opens 1♣, West bids 1◇, and North holds:

(1)　♠ K 8 4
　　　♡ J 10 7 6 4
　　　◇ 3
　　　♣ Q 9 5 2

Holding 5–7, he doubles. He will have an opportunity to show the heart suit later. Meanwhile, he establishes the range.

(2)　♠ Q J 4
　　　♡ K 7 5 2
　　　◇ A 3
　　　♣ 10 8 6 2

North has the technical requirements for 1NT, but the diamond guard is unsuitable for this call. It is better to cue-bid with 2◇ and see what develops.

(3)　♠ J 8 5
　　　♡ K Q 6 2
　　　◇ K J 4
　　　♣ Q 6 3

With 12 points and a double guard in diamonds, bid 2NT.

(c) When second hand overcalls with 1NT

This overcall will seldom be genuine – it may be a bluff with a long suit or it may, by agreement, show some form of 2-suiter. However, responder does not have to worry. He acts as follows:

With 0–4, pass.
With 5–7 and a balanced hand, double.
With 5–7 and a fair suit, bid the suit.
With positive values (8 upwards), always double first.

South opens 1♣, West overcalls with 1NT, and North holds:

(1)　♠ Q 10 8 7 5 3
　　　♡ K 4 3
　　　◇ 5
　　　♣ 10 8 5

45

Bid 2♠, showing a fair suit and a moderate hand.

(2) ♠ Q 5 2
   ♡ J 4
   ♢ Q 10 7 3
   ♣ 9 6 4 2

Holding 5–7 points and a balanced hand, double. This is a penalty double in principle.

(3) ♠ 7 4 2
   ♡ K 10 8 6 4 2
   ♢ A J 3
   ♣ 6

Although the hearts are strong, North's first action is to double. He does not expect the double to be passed out, but by doubling first, and bidding the suit later, he distinguishes between a hand with positive values and a moderate hand with a fair suit.

(d) When second hand overcalls at the two level

At this level, or higher, the system of responses must be reasonably flexible. In general, responder bids naturally, except that a double at the two level is not for penalties.

South opens 1♣, West overcalls with 2♡ (announced as weak), and North holds:

(1) ♠ J 4
   ♡ 10 7
   ♢ K J 9 6 3
   ♣ J 7 4 2

If North held one more diamond he might bid 3♢; as it is, a negative double is sounder.

(2) ♠ Q 5
   ♡ J 9 7 3 2
   ♢ 9 7 5 3
   ♣ J 2

North would like to double 2♡ for penalties, but one cannot have it both ways. The best move is to pass, hoping that partner will reopen with a take-out double, as he well may.

(3) ♠ Q J 7 5 3
      ♡ A 7 4
      ◇ 9 3
      ♣ 8 4 2

As he can bid his suit at the two level North should overcall with 2♠, forcing for one round.

(4) ♠ K 8 7 5
      ♡ 8 5
      ◇ A Q 6 4
      ♣ J 6 3

A double is preferable to a cue-bid of 3♡, which would lose too much bidding space.

The general system over intervention (other than 1NT) is straightforward and easy to remember: pass when weak, double when medium, otherwise retain the general structure of positive responses. The philosophy: don't go chasing butterflies in a field, making a series of penalty doubles at the end of which you won't know where you are. Stick to your own purposes and take advantage of the extra range of calls that the intervention provides.

Summary

(a) **Over a double by second hand** pass with 0–4, bid 1◇ with 5–7 and no 4-card major, redouble with 5–7 and at least one 4-card (or longer) major, give a normal positive response with 8 or more, or bid a semi-positive 2♡ or 2♠ with the usual values.

(b) **When second hand overcalls at the one level,** pass with 0–4, double (sputnik) with 5–7, bid 1NT on 8–10 with a suitable guard, with upwards of 8 and no guard either double with something in hand or cue-bid.

(c) **When second hand overcalls with 1NT,** pass with 0–4, double with 5–7 and a balanced hand, with 5–7 and a fair suit bid the suit, with positive values always double first.

(d) **When second hand overcalls at the two level** double is sputnik, suit bids may not be strong but are forcing for one round.

9 OPENING 1♦ AND RESPONSES

In previous versions of Precision the opening 1♦ has been described as 'natural, at least a 4-card suit'. If you follow that advice consistently, and combine it with 5-card majors, you are committed to opening 1NT on every balanced hand, without regard to 'texture'. The truth is that in any one club system 1♦ is something of a moveable feast. It takes care not only of hands in the 12–15 range which contain a genuine diamond suit, but also of many others which do not contain a 5-card major and are unsuitable for 1NT (13–15) or 2♣ (12–15 with a fair suit).

Opening types

These are some examples:

(1)   ♠ A 7 4
     ♡ A Q 8 3
     ♦ K 9 6 2
     ♣ 10 4

Open 1♦, not 1♡ on a 4-card suit. A response of 2♣ will not be embarrassing, because 2NT is available as a minimum rebid.

(2)   ♠ A K 7 5
     ♡ 6 2
     ♦ K 8 4
     ♣ A 8 6 2

Open 1♦ rather than 1♠ or 1NT. Opening bids on a 3-card suit are frequent.

(3)   ♠ A J 3
     ♡ 5
     ♦ A Q 8 2
     ♣ K 9 7 4 2

Open 1♦ rather than 2♣. With 4–5 in the minors 1♦ is usually correct, especially when the club suit is poor.

This is a slightly awkward hand for the system:

    (4) ♠ A 8 3
         ♡ A 7 5 2
         ◇ 9 4
         ♣ K Q 8 6

It is never correct to open 1◇ on a doubleton, so the only available opening is 1NT.

On many hands, however, 1◇ should be preferred to a sketchy 1NT.

    (5) ♠ K 7 5 3
         ♡ J 4
         ◇ Q 7 3
         ♣ A K 6 2

This hand qualifies in a sense for 1NT, but 1◇ is safer, especially when vulnerable.

(a) Response of 1♥ or 1♠

A response of 1♡ or 1♠ suggests in principle 7–15. As in all systems, the responder may sometimes lower the requirements for tactical reasons. Partner opens 1◇, vulnerable, and you hold:

    (1) ♠ Q 10 8 6 4 3
         ♡ K 6 3
         ◇ 4
         ♣ 9 6 2

Whatever you do could be wrong, but most players would bid 1♠ and hope to come out alive.

In any system which uses 5-card majors it is essential for responder, when not worth two constructive bids, to show a 4-card major at the one level. Otherwise the 4–4 fit is liable to be lost.

    (2) ♠ 7
         ♡ K J 6 3
         ◇ Q 4
         ♣ Q 10 9 6 4 2

Over 1◇ bid 1♡. If the opener rebids 1NT, it is safe to follow with 2♣; the sequence 1◇–1♡–1NT–2♣ can readily be dropped.

The situation is more awkward if partner rebids 1♠. You cannot hope now to play at the two level, for 1◇–1♡–1♠–2♣ is a constructive sequence. With 4–5 responder can bid 1NT over 1♠; with 4–6 he must choose between 1NT and 2♣, to be followed by 3♣.

This principle of responding in the short major does not extend to hands worth a response at the two level.

$$
\begin{array}{ll}
(3) & \spadesuit \ A \ Q \ 8 \ 4 \\
& \heartsuit \ 7 \ 5 \\
& \diamondsuit \ K \ 7 \\
& \clubsuit \ Q \ J \ 8 \ 4 \ 3
\end{array}
$$

Now develop in the normal way, bidding the longer suit first. The sequence 1◇–1♡–1NT (or 1◇–1♠–1NT) suggests a balanced 12–14. An opener who has a maximum 15 should aim to make a less limited rebid, either 2NT or 3◇ or a change of suit.

(b) Response of 1NT

This response suggests a balanced 8–10. The requirements may be shaded when four diamonds are held, a hand of this type:

$$
\begin{array}{l}
\spadesuit \ J \ 4 \\
\heartsuit \ Q \ 5 \ 2 \\
\diamondsuit \ K \ 10 \ 7 \ 3 \\
\clubsuit \ J \ 6 \ 4 \ 3
\end{array}
$$

As we will see shortly, a raise to 2◇ is constructive, and the trumps are not good enough for a pre-emptive raise to 3◇. The choice, therefore, lies between passing, which gives the opponents an easy chance to come in, and 1NT.

(c) Response of 2♣

Throughout the system a response at the two level promises fair values, usually 10 points upwards or 8–9 with a long, rebiddable suit.

$$
\begin{array}{ll}
(1) & \spadesuit \ Q \ 5 \ 3 \\
& \heartsuit \ 10 \ 6 \ 2 \\
& \diamondsuit \ 8 \ 4 \\
& \clubsuit \ A \ Q \ 6 \ 5 \ 3
\end{array}
$$

Respond 1NT, not 2♣.

(2)   ♠ K 6
♡ 7 3 2
◇ 4
♣ K Q 10 8 6 4 3

Respond 2♣ and follow with 3♣ on the next round. This is always a limited sequence.

The response of 2♣ is forcing as far as 2NT. This has a considerable bearing on the opener's rebids.

Opener's rebid after 1◇–2♣ (responder not having passed originally):

2◇
    May be a limited hand with rebiddable diamonds, but available also as a mark-time call when there is no good alternative, e.g.

♠ K 7 4 3
♡ 5 2
◇ A Q J 6
♣ K 8 2

2♡ 2♠
    These reverses suggest upper range and may be a notrump probe rather than a suit. Thus 2♠ is the best rebid on:

♠ A K 4
♡ 6 3
◇ A 8 7 5 3
♣ K 10 4

2NT
    A limited rebid consistent with a minimum opening, e.g.

♠ A 10 8
♡ Q 9 7 2
◇ K Q J 3
♣ 4 2

3♣
    Natural and non-forcing, usually good clubs.

3◇
    Good playing values in diamonds.

3♡ 3♠
    As 2♡ or 2♠ would be forcing, these jumps

signify good support for clubs with a control in the suit named. Rebid 3♡ on:

♠ 4
♡ A Q 6
◇ K Q 7 5 3
♣ A 10 8 4

3NT   Probably a maximum 15 with a guard in both majors.

For players not familiar with this style, the important points to remember are that 2♣ is forcing to 2NT, that 2NT is a minimum rebid, and that jumps in a new suit promise support for responder's suit. + controls

(d) Raises to 2♦ and 3♦

Precision uses 'inverted minor suit raises'; that is to say, a raise to 2◇ is stronger than a raise to 3◇.

This is an old idea of undoubted merit. It allows for gradual development on strong hands and for better defensive tactics on moderate hands with trump support.

The raise to 2◇ is equal to a 2-over-1 response, with a range of 10–15. This type of hand is difficult to manage in standard systems:

♠ A J 4
♡ 6 5
◇ A Q 8 3
♣ Q 8 4 2

The Precision response of 2◇ is forcing for one round and tends to deny a 4-card major.

After the raise to 2◇ the opener may either indicate a stopper (Q J x or better) in one major suit or bid notrumps when he guards both majors. If he does not hold a guard in either major he must rebid 3◇ (non-forcing) or 3♣.

The raise to 3◇ is a defensive bid similar to a double raise by third hand after a take-out double.

♠ K 7
♡ J 4
◇ Q 10 8 6 3
♣ 9 7 4 2

Raise 1◇ to 3◇. As the opener may have only three diamonds, five trumps, or four very good trumps such as K Q J 10, are necessary for this response.

(e) Responses of 2♥ 2♠ or 3♣

A jump in a new suit suggests slam possibilities and is always based either on a strong suit or on a fair suit with trump support. Respond 2♠ on either of these hands:

	(1)			(2)	
	♠	A K J 8 6 4		♠	A Q 7 6 3
	♡	9		♡	A J 5
	◇	K 6		◇	K J 9 4
	♣	A Q 5 3		♣	6

(f) Response of 2NT

This response serves for strong all-round hands from 16 upwards and is also the best first move on hands with very good trump support and no side suit. Respond 2NT on:

	(1)			(2)			(3)	
	♠	A 10 5 3		♠	K J 8 6		♠	K 5
	♡	K Q 4		♡	A J 8 2		♡	A J 4
	◇	Q 3		◇	6		◇	K J 9 7 5
	♣	A J 7 6		♣	A K 7 3		♣	K 10 8

The 2NT response is Baron, asking the opener to show 4-card suits upwards. Thus it is a good move on hand (2) above. Here is another example:

	West		*East*	
	♠	7	♠	A 10 6 2
	♡	A K 9 3	♡	J 8
	◇	K J 8 7 4	◇	A Q 9 2
	♣	Q 7 6	♣	A 8 5

The bidding goes:

West	*East*
1◇	2NT
3♡	3♠
3NT	4◇ (1)
6◇ (2)	pass

53

(1) East shows that his 2NT response was based on diamond support. The bidding can die in 4NT if West does not like the way things are developing.

(2) West has no great hand, but he has first or second round control of three suits and his partner has followed a strong sequence.

The play

North leads the queen of spades against six diamonds. All follow to the ace and king of trumps. Declarer could play South for the king of clubs, but a better chance is to lead a low heart towards the J 8. If North plays the queen dummy's clubs will go away on the A K of hearts. If North plays low without a quiver West puts in dummy's eight. At worst, this will lose to the ten, and declarer still has the option of playing South for the queen.

(g) Response of 3NT

As elsewhere in the system, 3NT indicates a balanced 14–15, usually 4–3–3–3.

When there is intervention over 1♦

When second hand doubles 1◇ the position is much the same as in standard systems. Suit bids by responder are non-forcing; 2NT conventionally shows a hand worth a sound raise to 3◇; direct raises are pre-emptive.

When second hand overcalls in a suit the following adjustments are made:

3◇ is now stronger than 2◇.
2NT is natural, about 11–13.

Double of intervention up to 2♣ is 'sputnik', and non-jump suit overcalls are accordingly non-forcing. Sputnik doubles are discussed in Chapter 12.

Summary

As an opening bid, 1◇ on a 3-card suit is often preferred to 1NT. With 4–5 in the minors, 1◇ is usually correct.

(a) **Response of 1♡ or 1♠.** The normal standard is 7–15 but this may be shaded with a long suit. On moderate hands with four of a major and a longer minor, responder bids the major suit first. A rebid of 1NT suggests 12–14.

(b) **Response of 1NT.** A balanced 8–10, sometimes shaded when four diamonds are held.

(c) **Response of 2♣.** Usually 10 points, may be 8–9 with a long, rebiddable suit. The sequence is forcing to 2NT. **Opener's rebids:** 2◇ may be a mark-time bid; 2♡ or 2♠ upper range, may be a notrump probe; 2NT balanced 12–13; 3♣ non-forcing; 3♡ 3♠ support for clubs and control in the suit named.

(d) **Raises to 2◇ and 3◇.** Raise to 2◇ 10–15, forcing for one round; raise to 3◇ defensive.

(e) **Response of 2♡ 2♠ or 3♣.** The jump-shift guarantees either a strong suit or a fair suit with good trump support.

(f) **Response of 2NT.** Either balanced 16 upwards, or strong 4–4–1–4, or very good trump support and no side suit. The response is Baron, asking for 4-card suits 'upwards'.

(g) **Response of 3NT.** Balanced 14–15, usually 4–3–3–3.

After intervention 3◇ is stronger than 2◇, 2NT is natural, double up to 2♠ is sputnik.

10 FIVE-CARD MAJORS AND THE FORCING NOTRUMP

The two standard-bearers of the Precision system are the opening 1♣ and the 5-card majors, with the response of 1NT forcing for one round. The two are not dependent on one another, but the fact that 1♡ and 1♠ are limited openings makes them easier to manage than in standard systems.

Why 5-card majors? And why should 1NT over 1♡ or 1♠ be forcing?

Any bidding system has two general objectives: one is to gain tactical advantage on competitive deals; the other, to enable the partnership to arrive at its best contract.

It is probably true that freedom to open 4-card majors confers a *slight* tactical advantage. You make it more difficult for the opponents to overcall; against that, the knowledge that opener has a 5-card suit is often helpful to responder when there is competition. A point often made in support of 4-card majors is that you don't run any risk of losing the 4–4 fits if you announce these suits on the first round; but this weakness, such as it is, in the 5-card major structure is almost entirely eliminated by the use of sputnik doubles (see Chapter 12).

When we turn to the other objective – that of bidding accurately to the best contract – the 5-card major system, with 1NT forcing for one round, has a *big* advantage. If you are doubtful of that, wait till you see how many extra shades of meaning can be expressed when you use 1NT as a relay. Before pursuing that theme we must take a brief look at the opening requirements for 1♡ or 1♠.

Opening standards

The normal standard is 12–15 points and a 5-card or longer suit. Apart from semi-psychic openings in third position the only time when a player may be tempted to open a 4-card major is when he holds this type:

♠ 842
♡ A Q J 3
♢ 94
♣ A K 10 5

Here 1♡ looks better than 1NT with two suits unguarded.

In case you are wondering what happens when opener has 4–4–1–4 distribution, those hands have a special treatment; see Chapter 15. 2 ♢

As in all systems, an 11-point hand with a good 6-card major represents a sound opening, and the same may be said of many 5–5–2–1 and 5–4–3–1 hands in the same range. Open 1♠ on any of the following:

(1) ♠ A Q 9 6 4 2   (2) ♠ K Q J 8 5   (3) ♠ A K 9 7 4
    ♡ 7   ♡ 4   ♡ K J 10 5
    ♢ A J 5   ♢ 76   ♢ 864
    ♣ 632   ♣ A J 9 5 2   ♣ 3

Types on which responder bids 1NT

Though forcing for one round, the response of 1NT is by no means necessarily strong. In many cases it corresponds to the moderate balanced hand on which one responds 1NT in a standard system. The response is made on four types:

1. Balanced or semi-balanced hands from 8 to 11, with from one to three cards in partner's suit.

2. Weakish hands with a long suit.

3. Hands worth a 'balanced raise', about 10 to 11 points with three cards in partner's suit and a ruffing value.

4. Good supporting hands with a special feature.

A much wider span, it will be observed, than is covered by 1NT in standard system. When a bid is forcing for one round it is surprising how the tree will spread.

Before giving examples of these responses we will examine the opener's rebid.

Opener's rebids over 1NT

When partner has made a bid that is capable of different meanings it is prudent to assume that he has one of the less cheerful types.

When rebidding over 1NT, therefore, opener should assume at first that responder is looking for a better fit or that he has a long suit in which he wants to play at the lowest possible level. The rebid is kept low except when there are solid playing values. These are the usual alternatives:

(a) **Opener names a second 4-card suit.**

      (1)   ♠ A Q 8 6 3
             ♡ K Q 2
             ♢ 4
             ♣ J 7 4 3

After 1♠–1NT rebid 2♣.

      (2)   ♠ A J 6 3
             ♡ K 10 7 5 2
             ♢ A 3
             ♣ J 6

After 1♡–1NT rebid 2♠. This reverse is not necessarily strong. Here the opener has no reasonable alternative. The bidding can die in 2NT or even in 2♠.

(b) **Opener with 5–3–3–2 names his lower minor.**

      (1)   ♠ K J 9 5 4
             ♡ A J 3
             ♢ Q 4 2
             ♣ K 8

After 1♠–1NT rebid 2♢. (A rebid of 2♡ always shows four.)

      (2)   ♠ A 8
             ♡ A Q 8 7 5
             ♢ A 9 4
             ♣ 7 6 3

After 1♡–1NT rebid 2♣. There is no need to be apprehensive about bidding this negligible suit. Partner will rarely pass, and when he does he will have at least four clubs and a singleton heart, in which case 2♣ may be a good stop.

(c) Opener with a 6-card suit or a strong 5-card suit rebids it.

$$(1) \quad \begin{array}{l} \spadesuit \; 6 \\ \heartsuit \; K J 10 8 6 3 \\ \diamondsuit \; K 7 5 \\ \clubsuit \; A 4 2 \end{array}$$

Rebid 2♡ rather than 2♣; but with 6–4 it is generally right to bid the second suit unless all the virtue of the hand lies in the long suit.

$$(2) \quad \begin{array}{l} \spadesuit \; A K Q 10 9 \\ \heartsuit \; K 8 7 \\ \diamondsuit \; 8 4 2 \\ \clubsuit \; J 3 \end{array}$$

Rebid 2♠, treating the spades as a 6-card suit.

(d) Opener with strong playing values makes a jump rebid

$$(1) \quad \begin{array}{l} \spadesuit \; K J 10 9 7 6 4 \\ \heartsuit \; A Q 8 \\ \diamondsuit \; K 5 \\ \clubsuit \; 4 \end{array}$$

Rebid 3♠. To make this jump rebid, the opener needs a powerful one-suited hand. On semi-2-suiters it is better to develop more slowly as partner may be wholly unsuitable for the main suit. Thus:

$$(2) \quad \begin{array}{l} \spadesuit \; A 7 \\ \heartsuit \; A Q 8 6 4 2 \\ \diamondsuit \; 4 \\ \clubsuit \; A 10 5 2 \end{array}$$

Rebid 2♣. It is a good hand but, as we shall see, partner may be weak, with a singleton heart and long diamonds; so, don't rush it.

(e) Opener with two strong suits jumps in his second suit

$$(1) \quad \begin{array}{l} \spadesuit \; 6 \\ \heartsuit \; A Q 10 8 4 3 \\ \diamondsuit \; A Q J 10 8 \\ \clubsuit \; 5 \end{array}$$

Rebid 3♢. This bid must be kept up to strength and both suits

59

must be good. It is wrong to jump on this type:

(2)   ♠ A K 7 6 2
         ♡ A 8
         ♢ 5
         ♣ K 9 7 6 2

Rebid 2♣. A jump to 3♣ would be a mistake for two reasons: the clubs are too weak and the hand is quite playable in hearts, should partner happen to hold length in that department.

(f) Opener with a set-up suit may rebid 2NT.

This rebid shows a hand playable at the three level in the major suit and also suitable for notrumps. Bid 2NT on:

(1)   ♠ A K Q 8 5 3   (2)   ♠ 10 3
      ♡ J 4 2   ♡ K Q J 9 7 5
      ♢ A 5   ♢ A 8 2
      ♣ 9 6   ♣ A 4

The type is known as BIG H (or BIG S).

Sequences following the response of 1NT

We look now at various sequences showing how responder acts on the second round.

1. Responder holds a balanced or semi-balanced 8–11.

1♡   1NT   A limited sequence, about 8–10 with two hearts,
2♣   2♡   or three hearts in a 4-3-3-3 hand, e.g.

                   ♠ Q 7 4
                   ♡ J 5
                   ♢ K 8 6 2
                   ♣ K 9 6 5

              or

                   ♠ A 8 2
                   ♡ 8 5 4
                   ♢ K J 8 5
                   ♣ 9 6 3

             With three trumps and a ruffing value it is normal to give a direct raise from one to two.

1♥ 1NT   Suggests 8–9 with short hearts and at least four
2♣ pass   clubs, e.g.

> ♠ 10763
> ♥ 6
> ♦ KJ95
> ♣ KQ64

Responder must bear in mind that opener may
well hold only three clubs. With a doubleton in
the major suit it is generally right to return to
the major.

1♠ 1NT   Should be at least five trumps, e.g.
2♦ 3♦

> ♠ 5
> ♥ K853
> ♦ Q10764
> ♣ A82

1♠ 1NT   This sequence expresses the 10–11 point hands
2♣ 2NT   that are difficult to bid accurately in standard
systems. Responder has this type:

> ♠ 64
> ♥ K1053
> ♦ AJ84
> ♣ Q92

The problem in a standard system is that you are
strong for 1NT and somewhat short of playing
strength for 2♦.

2. Responder holds a weakish hand with a long suit.

1♥ 1NT   Here responder introduces a new suit on the
2♣ 2♦   second round. This shows a limited hand with a
long suit and is known as TYPE L (for limited).
It will be a hand of this type:

> ♠ K65
> ♥ 4
> ♦ QJ10873
> ♣ 942

Playing a standard system, responder is in a familiar dilemma when his partner opens 1♡: 1NT has obvious disadvantages, 2◇ is unsound. At Precision there is no problem in reaching the right spot at a low level.

1♠ 1NT
2♣ 3♣

This is also Type L, but obviously the clubs must be very good as responder is fighting a long suit of spades. He has something like this:

♠ —
♡ J964
◇ 82
♣ KQJ8642

There are two sequences where a new suit by responder would *not* be Type L. These are when opener has made a jump rebid, either in his first suit or in a second suit.

(1) 1♡   1NT   (2) 1♠   1NT
     3♡   ?   3◇   ?

After these rebids responder would not attempt to argue. A new suit would be control-showing, probably the ace. Sequence (2) is not forcing and a simple return to 3♠ would imply dislike of the whole affair.

1♡ 1NT
2NT 3◇

This is Type L, but again the diamonds must be long and strong as opener is marked with good hearts and six or seven likely tricks in notrumps.

3. Responder holds a 'balanced raise', about 9 to 11 points with three cards in partner's suit and a ruffing value.

1♠ 1NT
2◇ 3♠

The values shown are similar to those expressed by jump preference in a standard system. Responder holds:

♠ Q75
♡ A863
◇ K842
♣ Q3

62

4. Responder holds a good supporting hand with a special feature.

1♡ 1NT 2any 4♡	This jump to game after 1NT shows very strong trumps, e.g. K Q x x x with an outside ace, or A K J x x with an outside king. The response is useful when opener has a powerful hand except for bad trumps, such as

♤ A Q x ♡ 10 9 x x x ◇ — ♧ A K J x x.

1♤ 1NT 2♧ 3◇	The <u>jump in a new suit after 1NT</u> signifies the <u>values for a raise to game with a singleton or void</u> <u>in the suit named</u>, e.g.

♤ K J 8 5
♡ A 9 6 4
◇ 5
♧ K Q 6 2

1♡ 1NT 2♧ 3NT	Now responder jumps in notrumps. That means that his shortage is in clubs, the suit partner has bid. He may hold:

♤ K 9 6 4 2
♡ A 8 7 5
◇ K J 5 2
♧ —

Obviously this information will be very welcome to an opener who has a fair hand but weak clubs, and it will warn of duplication when opener has strong clubs.

These last two sequences, where responder goes out of his way to stress a shortage in a side suit, are known as TYPE S (for singleton). We refer to them again when discussing the system of raises in the next chapter.

To recapitulate, the response of 1NT is made on the following classes of hand:

Moderate balanced hands, where 1NT would also be the response in a standard system.

Medium balanced hands, worth a natural 2NT.

Medium hands with three trumps and a doubleton, worth a double raise.

Moderate hands with a long suit.

Quite strong supporting hands, containing very good trumps or a shortage in a side suit.

Adjustments when responder is a passed hand

One of the commendable features of the Precision system is that for the most part bidding is conducted without reference to vulnerability or position at the table. In principle, 1NT by a passed hand is forcing and has one of the usual meanings. It must be recognized, however, that a player in third position, and to a lesser extent in fourth position, may open on a sub-minimum hand and be disposed to pass a response of 1NT lest partner follow on the next round with 2NT or a jump preference. It is sensible, therefore, to make the following adjustment:

When responder (having passed originally) has any type of balanced hand, and also when he has Type L, he bids 1NT in the normal way. But when he has strong trump support, or Type S, he bids 2NT. (This response is not needed in a natural sense because with 11–12 points responder can bid 1NT and follow with 2NT.)

Over 2NT, which now indicates the values for a raise to game opposite a sound opening, a player who has opened 1♡ rebids as follows:

3♣ 'Name your singleton, or bid 3♡ if you have none.'

3♢ 'I opened for a part score, and if you bid only 3♡ now I will pass.'

3♡ 'I haven't the shadow of an opening.'

4♡ 'Game is enough.'

When the opening bid is 1♠, 3♣ and 3♢ have the same meaning and 3♠ flashes the red light.

Summary

An opening 1♡ or 1♠ shows in principle a 5-card suit and 12 to 15 points, or 11 with good playing strength.

A response of 1NT is forcing and is made on the following types: balanced 8–11, 'balanced raise' (10–11 with a ruffing value), moderate hand with a long suit (TYPE L), certain types of strong supporting hand (see below).

Over 1NT opener names a second 4-card suit, bids his lowest 3-card suit with 5–3–3–2, rebids a 6-card suit, jumps in a new suit with two strong suits, or bids 2NT with a set-up suit.

When opener bids a new suit over 1NT responder may pass with a singleton of opener's suit and at least four cards in the second suit; may raise with at least five cards in the second suit; returns to opener's suit with a doubleton or three small in a moderate balanced hand; bids a new suit with length and moderate values (TYPE L); bids 2NT with 10 to 11; gives jump preference with three trumps, a doubleton, and 10–11. He expresses a strong supporting hand by jumping to game with very good trumps; by jumping to three of a new suit with a shortage in that suit; by bidding 3NT with a shortage in partner's second suit (TYPE S).

When opener makes a jump rebid in his own suit or in a new suit, responder with a weak hand may pass or give minimum preference. A new suit shows a control, not TYPE L.

When responder has passed originally he bids 1NT (still theoretically forcing) only on the balanced types or on TYPE L. With the strong supporting types he bids 2NT. Then opener bids 3♣, asking for the singleton if any, 3◇ with a minimum opening, three of his own suit as an unconditional sign-off, game in the suit with no higher aspirations

11 OTHER DEVELOPMENTS OVER 1♥ AND 1♠

Apart from the forcing 1NT, the responses to 1♥ and 1♠ are mostly analogous to those over 1◇, which we have already examined. We consider possible developments under these headings:

(a) When responder should pass.
(b) Response of 1♠ over 1♥.
(c) Response of two in a suit.
(d) Jump take-out.
(e) Response of 2NT.
(f) Response of 3NT.
(g) System of raises.
(h) When responder has passed originally.
(i) When there is intervention.
(j) Is it forcing?

(a) When responder should pass

It is generally advisable to pass on a balanced hand up to 7 points and on any bad hand, even if it contains a long suit. The situation is quite different from when partner has opened 1◇, which may be a short suit; here you know (or at any rate assume) that partner has a 5-card suit, so it won't be a disaster if you leave him in with a singleton.

(b) Response of 1♠ over 1♥

The requirements are much the same as in standard systems, from about 7 (less with a good suit) to 15.

(1) ♠ K J 10 7 5 3
     ♡ 4
     ◇ Q 4 2
     ♣ 9 7 5

You are under strength in terms of high cards but with a

singleton heart and rebiddable spades it is reasonable to respond
1♠.

$$(2) \quad \begin{array}{l} ♠ \ K9742 \\ ♡ \ 73 \\ ◇ \ QJ5 \\ ♣ \ 863 \end{array}$$

Now there is not much to be gained by responding, especially
as you can tolerate hearts.

As over 1◇, it is right to show a 4-card major in front of a
longer minor on a weak hand, but not when the responding hand
is worth two bids.

$$(3) \quad \begin{array}{l} ♠ \ AJ96 \\ ♡ \ 5 \\ ◇ \ K108743 \\ ♣ \ 72 \end{array}$$

Respond 1♠. If partner's rebid is 1NT he will let you play the
hand in 2◇.

$$(4) \quad \begin{array}{l} ♠ \ KQ94 \\ ♡ \ 63 \\ ◇ \ A10874 \\ ♣ \ K5 \end{array}$$

Now respond 2◇ as you are entitled to introduce the spades on
the next round.

After 1♡–1♠, 1NT by opener suggests 12–14; a change of suit
by opener is not forcing but is less limited; 2NT suggests 15 with
a guard in both minors.

(c) Response of two in a suit

A take-out at the two level is made on 10 upwards or 8–9 with a
rebiddable suit. A response of 2♡ promises five hearts. 2♣ and
2◇ may be approach bids on a 4-card suit. The normal way
to show a fairly balanced 12 points is to respond at the two level
and follow with 2NT; this sequence is slightly stronger than 1NT
followed by 2NT.

Opener's rebids after 1♡–2♣ (or similar)

2♡   Not forcing and not necessarily a 6-card suit, as
               opener may have no good alternative.

New suit   Forcing for one round and may not be a genuine suit.

> ♠ 6 3
> ♡ A Q 7 5 2
> ◇ A J 4
> ♣ K 8 3

After 1♡–2♣ bid 2◇ as a developing move. A reverse, 1♡–2♣–2♠, suggests upper range.

2NT   Limited balanced hand, with a presumption of at any rate a half-guard in the unbid suits, e.g.

> ♠ A J 5
> ♡ K Q 7 4 2
> ◇ Q 10 4
> ♣ 6 2

3♣   Not forcing, usually good clubs, such as:

> ♠ K 7
> ♡ A J 8 5 4
> ◇ 6 3
> ♣ K J 5 2

The sequence 1♠–2♡–3♡ is also not forcing.

Jump in new suit   Promises strong support for partner and a control in the suit named. Jump to 3◇ on:

> ♠ 4
> ♡ A Q 7 5 2
> ◇ A 7 5
> ♣ K Q 8 4

3♡   Good playing values in hearts, e.g.

> ♠ A 10 8
> ♡ K Q J 9 7 6
> ◇ K J
> ♣ 6 4

3NT   Maximum 15, with a guard in both the unbid suits.

(d) Jump take-out

As over 1◇, a jump take-out suggests upwards of 15 points and either a strong suit or good trump support and a fair suit. Responder shows the first type by rebidding his suit (or bidding notrumps) on the next round, the second type by supporting partner's suit.

When responder has a powerful hand but neither a set-up suit nor good support, his best action is to develop slowly, taking his cue from partner's rebids.

Opener bids 1♡ and responder holds:

(1)   ♠ K 6
      ♡ 7 4
      ◇ A Q 5
      ♣ A K Q 9 6 2

Force with 3♣, intending to follow with 3NT.

(2)   ♠ A 8 6
      ♡ K J 8 6
      ◇ A K 7 4 2
      ♣ 5

Force with 3◇ and support hearts on the next round.

(3)   ♠ A K 7 2
      ♡ 6 4
      ◇ A 8
      ♣ K Q J 6 3

Holding neither a powerful suit nor trump support, begin with 2♣. If partner makes a non-committal rebid such as 2◇, bid 2♠, still forcing of course, and wait for his next move; you are entitled to go as far as 4NT.

Follow the same tactics when you have *fair* support for partner and a *fair* side suit:

(4)   ♠ A J 5 2
      ♡ K 7 3
      ◇ A Q 8 5 3
      ♣ 4

A powerful hand in support of hearts, but again you lack either of the features that are expected from a force (strong suit or good trump support). You advance to game by bidding round the clock. Begin with 2◇ and, if space permits, show the spades and cue-bid the clubs on the way to 4♡. When a responder bids three suits before raising partner directly it usually means that his manoeuvres are based on trump support.

(e) Response of 2NT

This is a Baron response, 15 upwards, used on strong hands with no 5-card suit and also with strong support for partner's suit and no good side suit. Respond 2NT to 1♡ on any of the following hands:

(1)	♠ K96	(2)	♠ A75	(3)	♠ Q743
	♡ Q3		♡ KQ106		♡ 6
	◇ AQJ4		◇ K743		◇ AQ85
	♣ KQ63		♣ A8		♣ AK73

The response goes well on 4-4-4-1 hands because partner is requested to show his 4-card suits upwards until either a fit has been found or 3NT has been reached. As is well known, 4-4 fits tend to produce an extra trick. This objective may also be present when good support is held, as on these two hands:

	West	*East*
	♠ J5	♠ A6
	♡ AQ1076	♡ KJ52
	◇ KQ84	◇ AJ76
	♣ 63	♣ KQ5

The bidding goes:

West	*East*
1♡	2NT
3◇	3♡ (1)
3NT (2)	4◇
5◇ (3)	6◇ (4)
pass	

(1) East makes the maximum use of bidding space. There is no hurry to raise the diamonds.

(2) West might bid 4♡ but with a balanced minimum 3NT is more accurate. It suggests the 5–4–2–2 distribution.

(3) West has already signed off, and as his diamonds are respectable he advances in this suit.

(4) Correctly judging that it may be better to play in the 4–4 fit.

On a spade lead there is no play for 6♡. In 6◇ East's second spade will go away on the fifth heart and the contract is safe if trumps are 3–2.

When the opener has no second suit to show over the response of 2NT he rebids 3NT (limited 5–3–3–2 type) or repeats his first suit as a waiting bid. With a strong 2–suiter he can give an immediate picture by jumping in the second suit over 2NT.

(f) Response of 3NT

The response is made on balanced 14–15 or a reinforced 13. 3NT is not the most manageable of responses (I described it once as 'the most stultifying bid in the game') and should be restricted to specifically notrump types. Indeed, there is much to be said for making it a rule to respond 3NT only on 4–3–3–3 shape. The opener, with a moderate 5–4–3–1, can return to his own suit in the confidence of finding three trumps opposite. On 4–4–3–2 hands in this range it is always possible to make an approach bid in another suit.

(g) System of raises

Thanks mainly to the forcing response of 1NT, Precision has an imposing array of sequences to express support.

Single raise Much the same values, and tactical considerations, as in standard systems.

Double raise Again, a normal value bid. Playing 5-card majors, responder can freely raise on three trumps.

$$♠ 7$$
$$♡ 8\ 4\ 2$$
$$◇ A\ Q\ 8\ 6$$
$$♣ K\ 7\ 5\ 4\ 2$$

Raise 1♡ to 3♡. You could arrive at the same point by bidding 1NT and following with 3♡, or by beginning with 2♣, but as you are not going to find a better contract than hearts you might as well make the better competitive bid.

Direct raise to game A direct raise to game may be mainly pre-emptive. The upper range is higher than in standard systems because the opener's strength is limited.

West	East
♠ Q J 10 6 4	♠ A 8 7 5 2
♡ K 10 4	♡ 6
◇ A Q 5	◇ K J 7 3
♣ Q 6	♣ 8 4 2

With only three 'Neapolitan' controls (counting 2 for an ace, 1 for a king), East is not too strong for a direct raise of 1♠ to 4♠.

The play

North leads the king of clubs and follows with ace and another. Declarer should lead the king of hearts now, to smoke out the ace. If North turns up with ace of hearts in addition to the top clubs there is a good case for playing to drop a singleton king of spades.

1NT followed by a jump As we noted in the last chapter, 1NT followed by a jump in a new suit, or a jump in notrumps, indicates the values for a raise to game with a shortage (TYPE S). 1♠–1NT–2♣–3◇ shows a singleton (or void) diamond, 1♠–1NT–2♣–3NT a singleton club. This sequence is followed only on quite strong hands with upwards of four controls.

Swiss 4♣ and 4◇ Precision has its own variation of the well-known Swiss convention. A response of 4♣ indicates a sound raise to four containing no singleton or void, 4◇ the same but with emphasis on strong trumps.

(1) ♠ A 10 6 4
     ♡ K 8
     ◇ Q J 7
     ♣ A J 9 2

Over 1♠ bid 4♣, suggesting 5 to 6 controls with no singleton or void, trumps not better than A J x x.

(2) ♠ 5 2
     ♡ K Q 10 8
     ◇ K J 4
     ♣ A J 8 2

Over 1♡ bid 4◇, 'trump Swiss', suggesting 4 to 5 controls and good trumps, minimum K Q x x or K x x x x.

1NT followed by jump to game   This sequence, as noted in the last chapter, stresses exceptional trump support.

2NT followed by support   As noted in section (e) above, this sequence takes care of balanced hands too strong for Swiss 4♣ or 4◇.

Delayed game raise   This technique, familiar to Acol players, is used when the responder has a fair side suit and good trump support. Responder first bids his suit and then jumps to game in the opener's suit. These are all d.g.r. sequences:

(1) 1♡ 2◇   (2) 1♡ 2♣
     3◇ 4♡   2NT 4♡

(3) 1♠ 2◇   (4) 1♠ 2♣
     2♡ 4♠   2♠ 4◇

In (4) a raise to 4♠ would be a normal value bid; to show d.g.r. responder jumps in the opposite minor.

The technique is useful on hands where twelve tricks can be run so long as the necessary controls are held.

West	East
♠ K Q 9 5 2	♠ A J 6 3
♡ J 7 4	♡ 3
◇ A 10 6	◇ 8 2
♣ Q 7	♣ A K 8 6 4 3

The bidding goes:

West	East
1♠	2♣
2NT	4♠ (1)
5◇ (2)	6♠ (3)
pass	

(1) 3♠ at this point would be forcing, so 4♠ is
d.g.r.

(2) West's ace of diamonds and queen of clubs
now become very important cards, so he shows
his control in diamonds.

(3) ... Which is just what East wanted to hear.

The play

The defenders begin with two rounds of hearts,
forcing dummy to ruff. West draws two trumps
with the ace and king, finding the trumps 3–1. At
this point he should switch to queen and ace of
clubs. If the clubs are 4–1 there is the extra chance
of finding the same player with four clubs and
the outstanding trump. This will allow the declarer to establish the clubs and re-enter dummy
with the third round of spades.

(h) When responder has passed originally

As explained in the last chapter, 1NT by a passed hand is still
forcing in theory but is liable to be passed by an opener who is
minimum or sub-minimum. When he has one of the supporting
types responder bids 2NT (not needed as a Baron bid).

A take-out into a new suit at the two level is not forcing but suggests fair values. With a weak hand and a long suit responder can still employ TYPE L (1NT first, then the suit).

A jump in a new suit, as at Acol, shows a fair holding in the suit plus the values for a raise to three at least. Third hand opens 1♤ and responder holds:

$$♤ \ Q\,10\,7\,4$$
$$♡ \ 5$$
$$♢ \ 9\,6\,3$$
$$♧ \ A\,K\,7\,4\,2$$

He jumps to 3♧. If opener is up to strength he must rebid 4♤, not 3♤, which would be a sign-off.

(i) When there is intervention

When there is intervention over 1♡ or 1♤, responses of 1NT and 2NT are natural. The usual understandings exist over a take-out double.

Swiss responses retain their normal meaning when there is a jump to 4♧ or 4♢. Thus 1♤–2♡ (intervention) – 4♧ would be Swiss and so would 1♡–2♢–4♢.

A double of intervention up to 2♤ is natural opposite a third or fourth hand opening, sputnik when the opening was in first or second hand. For an account of sputnik doubles, see the next chapter.

(j) Is it forcing?

Before leaving the general subject of responses to 1♡ and 1♤ it may be well to check on which sequences are forcing and which are not, as misunderstandings in this respect are the commonest source of disaster.

There is a tendency in Precision to treat some sequences as forcing that in the past (at any rate in the Acol system) have not been so regarded. That is partly because Precision has many ways of expressing moderate hands; it is also in line with the policy I mentioned before – that of not being afraid to go one range higher so long as you play eventually in the best strain.

The majority of 'mixed' sequences are forcing at the three level.

These are some examples:

| (1) | 1♡ | 1♠ | (2) | 1♠ | 2◇ | (3) | 1♡ | 2♣ |
| | 2♠ | 3♡ | | 2NT | 3♠ | | 3♣ | 3♡ |

The first two sequences would be forcing in any modern system. The third was not forcing in 'old-fashioned Acol' but is forcing in Precision as it would otherwise be difficult to develop certain hands. An advantage of 3♡ being forcing is that opener, having already limited his hand, has room to show an additional feature below game level.

When the opening bid is 1◇ sequences analogous to those above are likewise forcing. Thus 1◇–1♡–2♡–3◇ is forcing.

When the rebid is 1NT a jump in partner's first suit is forcing only when both majors are involved.

| (4) | 1♡ | 1♠ | (5) | 1◇ | 1♡ |
| | 1NT | 3♡ | | 1NT | 3◇ |

Sequence (4) is forcing as far as 3♠. Sequence (5) can be passed.

When opener has bid two suits preference or jump preference at the three level is forcing only when the first response was at the level of two and opener has reversed – in other words, when both players have bid constructively.

| (6) | 1♠ | 2♣ | (7) | 1◇ | 1♠ |
| | 2◇ | 3♣ | | 2♡ | 3◇ |

These are not forcing because only one of the partners has bid constructively. In (6) East has responded at the two level but West's 2◇ was a neutral rebid. In (7) West has reversed but East has only responded at the one level. But the next two sequences are forcing:

| (8) | 1♡ | 2♣ | (9) | 1♠ | 2♡ |
| | 2♠ | 3♡ | | 3♣ | 3♠ |

In (8) West has reversed and East has responded at the two level. (A raise to 3♠ would also be forcing.) In (9) opener's rebid at the three level counts as a reverse in this context.

As in all modern systems, a new suit at the three level is forcing except in a few situations where it is clear that both players are limited (e.g. 1◇–1♡–2◇–2NT–3♣); so is a reverse by responder in a sequence such as 1◇–1♡–2◇–2♠, and also 1◇–1♡–1NT–2♠.

Be sure to master this section and avoid those famous last words, 'I never thought you'd pass'. Apart from that, slam bidding proceeds much more easily when you can be sure that the engine won't break down.

Summary

(a) **Pass** on a balanced hand up to 7 and on any bad hand.

(b) **Respond 1♠ over 1♡** from 7 (less with a good suit) to 15. Rebid of 1NT suggests 12–14, 2NT 15; a change of suit is not forcing. On moderate hands a 4-card major is bid in preference to a longer minor.

(c) **Response at the two level** promises 10 upwards or 8–9 with a rebiddable suit. 1♠–2♡ shows a 5-card suit. A rebid by opener in his own suit is not forcing. A change of suit is forcing for one round. A rebid of 2NT shows 12–14, 3NT 15. A raise of partner's suit is not forcing. Jump in a new suit promises strong support and a control in the suit named.

(d) **Jump take-out** suggest upwards of 15 and either a strong suit or good trump support and a fair suit.

(e) **Response of 2NT** is Baron, 15 upwards with no 5-card suit. Opener shows 4-card suits 'upwards', or rebids 3NT with limited 5–3–3–2, or repeats his first suit, or jumps with two good suits.

(f) **Response of 3NT** is made on 14–15, preferably 4–3–3–3.

(g) **Special raises:** As noted in the last chapter, 1NT followed by a jump in a new suit or in notrumps indicates the values for a raise to game with a shortage (TYPE S). 1NT followed by a jump to game denotes very strong trumps. Swiss 4♣ indicates a sound raise to four containing no singleton or void, 4◇ the same with good trumps, minimum K Q x x or K x x x x. Responder with a fair side suit and good trump support makes a delayed game raise, bidding his suit and then raising to game; when opener rebids his own suit at the two level responder jumps to 4♣ (or, if clubs have been bid, to 4◇) to express d.g.r. values.

(h) When responder has passed originally a take-out at the two level is not forcing but suggests fair values. A jump take-out shows strength in the suit and the values for a raise to three at least. As noted in the last chapter, the response of 1NT is still forcing in principle but is made only on the balanced types or on TYPE L, not with strong supporting hands.

(i) When there is intervention over 1♡ or 1♤, responses of 1NT and 2NT are natural. Swiss responses retain their usual meaning when made with a jump. A double of intervention up to 2♤ is sputnik when the opening was in first or second hand, otherwise for penalties.

(f) These sequences are forcing: When responder's suit is raised and responder returns to opener's suit at the three level; when responder bids at the two level and returns to partner's suit over 2NT; when the rebid is 1NT and responder jumps to 3♡ (both major suits having been called); when opener has reversed and responder, having bid at the two level, gives preference; a new suit at the three level unless both players are limited; a reverse by responder.

12 SPUTNIK DOUBLES

The so-called 'negative' or 'sputnik' double has been around for a long time, as may be gathered from its name: it was devised when the first sputnik was in the news. The reason why players have been slow to adopt this style, despite its obvious advantages, is that until recently the doubles have not been properly defined.

As the reader has no doubt gathered from previous references, if not from his own experience, when sputnik doubles are played the double of intervention at the level of one or two is usually not for penalties but denotes general values. For Precision players, using 5-card majors, sputnik doubles are more or less indispensable. We consider them under these headings:

(a) When is a double sputnik?
(b) On what type of hand is a sputnik double made?
(c) How does the opener rebid?
(d) Doubles at the three level.

(a) When is a double sputnik?

This is easily stated:

After an opening 1◊ any double of intervention (apart from 1NT) up to the level of 2♠ is sputnik.

After an opening 1♡ or 1♠ by first or second hand any double up to the level of 2♠ is sputnik. When 1♡ or 1♠ is opened by third or fourth hand, double is for penalties; the reason for the distinction is that when responder has passed he can make a non-forcing suit response, and that makes the sputnik double less valuable.

(b) On what type of hand is a sputnik double made?

The simplest answer is that you make a sputnik double when you would otherwise be stuck for a bid. The bidding begins:

South	West	North	East
1◊	1♠	?	

As North you hold:

♠ 743
♡ K J 10 2
♦ J 3
♣ K 642

A response of 2♣ or 2♡ is unattractive, and if you pass you may get the worse of a part-score hand; you may even miss game in hearts. A sputnik double solves your problem. It conveys this message:

'I have a moderate hand in the range of 8 to 10, including four cards in the other major.'

Some more examples follow, after different sequences. South opens 1♦, West overcalls with 1♡, and North holds:

♠ Q 9 6 3
♡ J 4
♦ Q 7 2
♣ A 8 5 4

North could bid 1♠, but a sputnik double gives a better picture of the all-round values. Note that, again, four cards are held in the 'other major'.

South opens 1♡, West overcalls with 1♠, and North holds:

♠ 10 7 4
♡ 6 5
♦ A Q 6 3
♣ K 6 5 3

Again, a sputnik double expresses just what North wants to say: 'I can't bid notrumps, I can't support hearts, but I have some values and am playable in either of the unbid suits.'

These doubles are equally useful at the two level. South opens 1♦, West makes a weak jump overcall of 2♡, and North holds:

♠ K 7 5
♡ 6 4
♦ A 8 2
♣ Q 10 7 5 3

The best that North can do is double. At this level there is not the same guarantee of four cards in the other major.

South opens 1♠, West overcalls with 2♣, and North holds:

♠ 9 6
♡ K 10 8 5
♢ A Q 4
♣ 7 5 3 2

Again, a sputnik double is the best solution.

Some players would fancy a penalty double on the hand above Suppose that North has much stronger defence, as here:

♠ 5
♡ K 8 4 2
♢ A 5 3
♣ Q 10 8 5 3

This example brings us to a question that may have already occurred to the reader: what do you do when you have a whopping penalty double?

The answer, in most cases, is that responder who has a promising penalty double should pass, hoping that his partner will be able to reopen. The corollary to this is that the opener, when the bidding reverts to him, should be much more ready to reopen, especially with a double, than is normal. Pursuing the example above, the bidding begins:

South	West	North	East
1♠	2♣	pass	pass
?			

South holds:

(1) ♠ A Q 7 6 4
    ♡ A J 5
    ♢ Q 9 6 2
    ♣ 2

Although his opening is little more than minimum, South should double, for it seems very likely that his partner is lying in wait. (South may, of course, be deterred from this course if East has given obvious consideration to making a bid over 2♣.)

Still with the same sequence, South holds:

(2) ♠ K Q 8 6 3
    ♡ A 5
    ♢ Q J 9 8 4
    ♣ 2

Most players would pass, afraid of stirring up a hornet's nest. Playing sputnik doubles, you don't take that view. You assume that partner has most of the undeclared strength and reopen in this case with 2◊. If you were slightly stronger, even with the king of diamonds instead of the queen, you would consider a double.

It may appear, on the surface, that the overcaller's partner could trap the opener by passing on a good hand. All one can say is that it doesn't seem to happen like that. It would be a risky manoeuvre, for South, with some length in the enemy suit, might conclude that his partner was not lying in wait and might pass.

When the responder feels that he is too strong to adopt waiting tactics he can either bid notrumps or double first and follow with 2NT or 3NT.

It may happen, on rare occasions, that you will miss, or think you have missed, an 1100 penalty because you could not double for penalties. In that connection I recall an observation by the Italian authors of the book on the Blue Club. 'We don't worry about failing to beat par', they said in effect. 'We are concerned only with not falling short of our own par.'

As this question of missing fat penalty doubles seems to rankle with some players, it is worth remarking that these things tend to balance out. Consider this hand from a world championship match where East-West held at game all:

	West		East
♠	A K 9 6 3	♠	7 4
♡	Q J 10 8	♡	5
◊	10 4	◊	K J 8 6 3
♧	Q 2	♧	A 9 5 4 2

West opened 1♠ and North, who had six hearts to the A K, over-called with 2♡. East made a sputnik double. Judging that his partner would have strength in both minors, West passed and picked up 500, while at the other table the same contract was undoubled.

(c) How does the opener rebid?

The opening bidder seldom has any problem in choosing his rebid when responder has made a sputnik double at the one level.

Suppose, first, that he has opened 1◇ and an opponent has overcalled in a major suit.

South	West	North	East
1◇	1♡	dble	pass
?			

South assumes that his partner has a limited hand in the 8 to 10 range, including four spades. This is how he rebids with various types of hand:

(1) ♠ J 64
♡ 63
◇ A J 8 5 2
♣ A K 4

Rebid 1♠.

(2) ♠ A 10 7 4
♡ 3
◇ K 9 8 6 4
♣ A J 5

Rebid 2♠, just as though partner had responded 1♠.

(3) ♠ 76
♡ A Q 9 8
◇ K Q 5 2
♣ Q 10 6

Rebid 1NT. Do not be tempted to pass the double for penalties.

(4) ♠ 75
♡ A Q 4
◇ A K J 9 4 3
♣ J 2

Rebid 2NT, trusting partner to hold the black suits.

(5) ♠ Q 4
♡ 72
◇ A Q 10 9 7 4
♣ A J 5

Rebid 3◇.

(6) ♠ K J 4
♡ 6
◇ A K 8 6 3
♣ A 8 5 2

Rebid 2♡, the opponent's suit, ensuring that you have time to develop what looks like a game-going hand.

When the overcall is at the two level the rebid is sometimes a more delicate affair, because now you have not the same information about partner's suit-lengths. The bidding begins:

South	West	North	East
1♧	2♣	dble	pass
?			

South holds:

(1)   ♤ A J 8 6 5
          ♡ A 8 4
          ◇ A 6
          ♧ 8 5 3

Although there is no guarantee that partner holds four hearts South should rebid 2♡ rather than 2♤, as it is already known that he holds five spades. If North in fact has only three hearts he will transfer to 2♤ on a doubleton.

(2)   ♤ A K 10 7 4 3
          ♡ A J 6 2
          ◇ Q
          ♧ 7 3

This could be a powerful hand in either spades or hearts. Rather than plunge in either suit, South should bid 3♧ and see what this produces.

(d) Doubles at the three level

A double of intervention at the three level is best described as 'co-operative'. The double is in principle for penalties but should not be based on trump tricks alone. With Q 10 9 x of the opponent's suit and not more than a king outside, it is advisable to pass. When the double does not suit the opener's hand he should feel free to remove it in the assurance that partner will produce some tricks outside the trump suit.

Summary

After an opening 1◇ a double of intervention is sputnik up to the level of 2♧. After an opening 1♡ or 1♧ double up to 2♧ is sputnik only when the opener was in first or second hand.

A sputnik double at the one level suggests 8 to 10 points with four cards in the other major. Opener makes natural rebids on that basis. To force, he must make a cue-bid in the opponent's suit.

A sputnik double at the two level suggests similar values but does not give rise to the same distributional inferences.

When a double would be sputnik a responder who has a natural penalty double should usually pass. The first player should be prepared to reopen even on a minimum.

A double at the three level is in principle for penalties but should not be based on trump tricks alone.

Note. The scheme of sputnik doubles described in this chapter does not represent the last word. The doubles can be extended to stronger hands. When responder has the values for a response at the two level he doubles first and introduces his suit on the next round. This is called a 'High Power' double, as opposed to the 'Low Power' doubles described above. The advantage of the method is that suit overcalls by responder, in a sequence such as 1◇–1♧ (intervention)–2♡, become non-forcing, which is often convenient. Readers who want to study this treatment will find a fuller account in *Tiger Bridge*, by Jeremy Flint and Freddie North.

13 OPENING 1NT

The range for 1NT is 13–15 at any score and in any position. Many players these days bid a 12–14 notrump even when vulnerable against not. I personally consider that foolhardy and have many 800s in my pocket to prove it. Thus my advice is that with 13, vulnerable, 1◇ should be preferred so long as at least three diamonds are held.

A 5-card minor suit, in a 5–3–3–2 hand, is no bar to 1NT, but it is not systemic to conceal a 5-card major.

There are, of course, many systems of responses to 1NT. At rubber bridge most players use 2♣ as Stayman and leave it at that, but tournament players tend to use more sophisticated methods. Some use low-level transfers, which can become quite complicated. Another method is to use 2◇ as 'constructive Stayman', 2♣ as 'gladiator', requiring partner to respond 2◇ and developing from there in different directions.

A partnership that has a settled and satisfactory system need not change it when taking up Precision. However, a very good scheme can be based on the 'official' Precision method, in which 2♣ is non-forcing Stayman and 2◇ forcing Stayman. The remaining responses can be dealt with quite quickly.

(a) General schedule of responses

Responses to 1NT (13–15)

2♣	Non-forcing Stayman, see below for full treatment.
2◇	Forcing Stayman, see below for full treament.
2♡ 2♠	Weak responses.
2NT	Natural, 10–11.
3♣ 3◇	Pre-emptive. Jump to 3♣ on:

$$
\begin{array}{l}
\spadesuit\ 9\,5\,4\,2 \\
\heartsuit\ 6 \\
\diamondsuit\ K\,3 \\
\clubsuit\ J\,10\,8\,7\,4\,2
\end{array}
$$

3♡ 3♠   Invitational, a good suit not requiring trump support. Jump to 3♡ on:

         ♠ K 4
         ♡ Q J 10 9 5 3
         ◇ K 64
         ♣ 8 2

      Opener is invited to bid game unless markedly short of high cards.

4♣ 4◇   Transfer bids to 4♡ and 4♠ respectively.

Alternatively, those for whom the road to every slam is paved with Blackwood may prefer to use 4♣ as ace inquiry, the Gerber convention. Opener then bids 4◇ with no aces, 4♡ with one, and so forth.

(b) 2♣ as non-forcing Stayman

The response of 2♣ is treated by opener as normal Stayman. Opener bids 2♡ or 2♠ with four (2♡ first with 4–4), and otherwise 2◇. However, the responder is not always concerned with finding a major-suit fit. He may begin with 2♣ for any of the following purposes:

1. In pursuit of a 4–4 fit. Depending on his values, responder may intend to play at a low level or to make a try for game, or to follow with 2NT (natural). A sequence such as 1NT–2♣–2♡–3♣ suggests 4–6 in the black suits; responder has bid 2♣ in the hope of finding a spade fit. 1NT–2♣–2◇–3◇ conventionally asks the opener to name a 3-card major.

2. As an escape hatch. Partner opens 1NT vulnerable, the next hand passes, and you hold:

         ♠ 9 5 4
         ♡ K 86
         ◇ J 74
         ♣ 8 6 5 3

You know you are outgunned and it is good tactics to bid 2♣. You expect to lose 200 or so wherever you settle, but it is much harder for the opponents to nail you for 500 than if you pass and let them begin with a double of 1NT.

3. As an invitational move. To begin with 2♣ and follow with a free bid in a major suit is an invitational sequence, useful particularly on 5–4–3–1 hands that are difficult to value. For example, you hold:

> ♠ K 10 8 6 4
> ♡ 5
> ♢ A J 7 2
> ♣ J 5 3

You respond 2♣ and over a rebid of 2♢ or 2♡ you bid 2♠. If partner has a fair hand in support of spades he will advance in some direction.

The sequence may also be followed on more balanced hands containing a 5-card major.

West	East
♠ J 10 4	♠ A 7 5
♡ K 6 5	♡ A J 7 4 2
♢ A 8 6 2	♢ J 5 4
♣ A K 2	♣ 10 6

The bidding goes:

West	East
1NT	2♣ (1)
2♢	2♡
2NT (2)	3NT
pass	

(1) East has the values for a raise to 2NT, but the invitational sequence, in which the hearts are mentioned, is better.

(2) As West is maximum, with a fair holding in hearts, he accepts the proposition.

The play

North leads a low spade to South's king. A spade is returned and the jack is covered by the queen and ace. West needs only four tricks now from the hearts. He should play low to the king and duck the next round if North follows suit, ensuring four tricks. It would be right to duck even if North played the queen on the second round, as this might be a clever false card from Q 10 9 x.

4. As a stronger invitation. Except when opener rebids 2♠ over 2♣, responder has room in which to extend a still stronger invitation by jumping in his major suit. After 1NT–2♣–2◇ jump to 3♠ on:

> ♠ K J 7 6 4 2
> ♡ A 8
> ◇ J 9 6 3
> ♣ 5

The difference between this sequence and a direct jump to 3♠ is that responder now is more interested in finding some trump support.

(c) 2♦ as forcing Stayman

Although 2◇ is described as forcing Stayman, the situation really is that 2◇ is a game force to which opener responds in the first place by showing a 4-card major, or by bidding 2NT, or possibly 3♣ or 3◇ with a 5-card minor.

The use of 2◇ as a game force allows for gradual development and is particularly helpful when responder's main strength is in the minors; those hands are often difficult to explore in other systems.

West	East
♠ J	♠ A 8 5
♡ A 7 4	♡ K J 6 2
◇ K Q 7 6 3	◇ A 8
♣ A K 9 2	♣ J 10 7 3

East is the dealer. It is not unknown for such hands to be played in 3NT and for declarer to be unable to find a ninth trick in time after a spade lead. At Precision the bidding goes:

West	East
—	1NT
2◇	2♡
3◇	3NT
4♣ (1)	4♠ (2)
6♣ (3)	

(1) West follows the principle I have mentioned more than once: don't be afraid to go one higher in search of the best strain.

(2) As East has trump support and top cards, and has signed off in 3NT, he is entitled to cue-bid his ace. It is usual to cue-bid the lowest ace, but here 4◇ would sound like preference for diamonds.

(3) Having gone so far, West is going to see it through.

The play

It is not so easy to decide on the best plan in 6♣ after a spade lead, taken by the ace. To play off ace and king of clubs, followed by the top diamonds, will doubtless be good enough if trumps are 3–2, but a 4–1 break will be awkward. The best line may be to lead a low club and finesse the nine at trick two. If this loses to the queen and a trump is returned, win with the ten, ruff a spade, cross to the king of hearts, ruff a spade, cross to ace of diamonds and draw the last trump. West still has ace of hearts and K Q x x of diamonds, and there is a trump on the table for a diamond ruff if the suit does not break.

When the bidding begins 1NT–2◇–2NT, opener is presumed to hold no 4-card major or 5-card minor. A rebid of 3♣ by responder asks for exact shape. Opener bids 3◇ with 3-3-4-3, 3♡ with 2-3-4-4, 3♠ with 3-2-4-4, 3NT with 3-3-3-4; a display of exactitude that will daunt the opposition.

Summary

The range for an opening 1NT is 13–15 in all positions. When vulnerable, 1◇ may be safer on a minimum hand.

There are two conventional responses, 2♣ and 2◇. 2♣ is non-forcing Stayman and is used also when responder wants to make an invitational move in a major suit. 2◇ is game-forcing; opener shows a 4-card major or a 5-card minor, or bids 2NT, with the possible continuations described above on this page.

Other responses: 2♡ and 2♠ weak, 2NT natural, 3♣ 3◇ pre-emptive, 3♡ 3♠ invitational with strong trumps, 4♣ and 4◇ transfers to 4♡ and 4♠ respectively.

14 OPENING 2♣

Any system which uses 1♣ as a conventional opening must find an alternative, presumably 2♣, for limited hands containing a club suit. This is a delicate area in all one club systems, because of the lack of bidding space before the critical point of 3NT is reached. In Precision, where the 2♣ opener is liable to have a 4-card major on the side, the problem is greater than in systems where 2♣ will always be a one-suited hand.

It is sound policy, therefore, to restrict the opening to as narrow a range as possible. This is partly because accurate bidding is more difficult when you start at the two level, and partly because, the narrower the confines of the bid, the better chance you have of overcoming the difficulty.

Opening types

The opening 2♣ shows, in principle, a hand in the 12–15 range containing a fair club suit. As will be gauged from the patter above, when there is a reasonable alternative to 2♣ one takes it. So let us look, first, at some hands where 2♣ is *not* the recommended opening.

$$
\text{(1)} \quad
\begin{array}{l}
\spadesuit\ 7 \\
\heartsuit\ K\,8\,4 \\
\diamondsuit\ A\,J\,9\,2 \\
\clubsuit\ K\,Q\,9\,7\,5
\end{array}
$$

With 4–5 in the minors prefer 1◇ unless the diamonds are negligible and the clubs so strong that you can treat them as a 6-card suit.

$$
\text{(2)} \quad
\begin{array}{l}
\spadesuit\ K\,J\,5 \\
\heartsuit\ 7\,4 \\
\diamondsuit\ A\,10\,8 \\
\clubsuit\ A\,Q\,10\,4\,2
\end{array}
$$

An opening 2♣ is unlikely to be fatal, but the responses and rebids are not geared to this 5-3-3-2 distribution. If it pains you (as it does me) to open 1NT with a small doubleton in a major suit, there is nothing wrong with 1◇. (It follows from these two examples that when a player opens 1◇ and follows with a bid of clubs, there is an assumption that his clubs will be at least as good as his diamonds.)

(3) ♠ 6 2
     ♡ A K J 4
     ◇ K 5
     ♣ Q 8 7 4 2

Here the hearts are strong and the clubs weak. The roof won't fall in if, for once, you open 1♡ on a 4-card suit.

(4) ♠ K 6 3 2
     ♡ A Q 4
     ◇ 5
     ♣ A 8 6 3 2

One need not be over-solicitous about opening 2♣ on a moderate suit, but here there is a good alternative. As we will see in the next chapter, an opening 2◇ takes care of 3–4–1–5 and 4–3–1–5 hands in this range.

Having noted these alternatives we find that the opening 2♣ can be narrowed down to three types:

A. Hands with six clubs where, in a standard system, one would open 1♣ and rebid 2♣, e.g.

     ♠ K 5
     ♡ 8 3
     ◇ K 9 4
     ♣ A Q J 8 6 4

B. Hands with five clubs and four of a major, but not a singleton in diamonds, e.g.

     ♠ K Q 7 4   ♠ 7 3
     ♡ 5   ♡ A Q 9 5
     ◇ A 6 3   ◇ 6 2
     ♣ K Q 8 7 4   ♣ A K J 7 3

C. Shapely 2-suiters with four of a major and six clubs, or four diamonds and six clubs, e.g.

♠ K J 3 2	♠ 6
♡ 4	♡ J 5
◇ A 8	◇ A K 8 4
♣ A Q 10 7 5 3	♣ A J 9 7 4 2

Putting it still more briefly, the opener is marked with a 6-card club suit or a 5-card suit with four cards of a major.

Schedule of responses

It is essential to play 2◇ as a relay asking for information about the opener's type. All other responses are natural and do not require much comment.

Responses to 2♣

Pass Generally correct on a flat hand up to 8 points and on any hand up to 7 points unless it contains good support for clubs.

> ♠ 6 2
> ♡ Q 10 8 6 5 4
> ◇ A 9 6 3
> ♣ 4

Pass, for although 2♡ is not forcing and may be a better spot than 2♣, it is unsound to invite partner to continue.

> ♠ K J 3
> ♡ 8 5 2
> ◇ A 7 5 2
> ♣ 6 4 2

Pass, as it is difficult to visualize a game.

2◇ A relay, see below for full treatment.

2♡ 2♠ A 5-card or longer suit, invitational but not forcing, 8–11 points.

> ♠ K Q 9 7 6 4
> ♡ 2
> ◇ K 7 4 3
> ♣ 6 5

93

Bid 2♠, as there might be game in the suit.

♠ J52
♡ AQJ53
♢ QJ5
♣ 74

Bid 2♡. You have a maximum in high cards, but game is not certain.

Over this response of two in a major the opener (if not passing) rebids naturally. The most discouraging rebid is 3♣.

2NT   Natural, 10–12, with guards in the majors but no length.

3♣   Constructive raise, but not forcing, e.g.

♠ A75   ♠ 4
♡ J3   ♡ A82
♢ A9742 ♢ 108753
♣ 643   ♣ K952

This response, like 2NT, tends to deny a 4-card major.

3♢   Good diamond suit, such as A K 10 9 x x x, not much else.

3♡ 3♠   These are strongly invitational, showing the sort of values on which in a standard system a player would make a jump rebid, e.g.

♠ A4
♡ KQJ953
♢ Q74
♣ 84

3NT   To play, about 13–16, may be less with a fit for clubs.

4♣ 5♣   Mainly defensive, with distributional support.

The response of 2♦

The response of 2♢ is forcing for one round and is made on possible game hands that do not fit into the schedule above.

Before looking at hands suitable for the response it may be helpful to glance at the opener's rebids, which are straightforward except that a partly conventional meaning attaches to 2NT.

Opener's rebids after 2♣–2◇

2♡ 2♠	A second suit of four cards.
2NT	No 4-card major; probably six clubs and a stopper in two side suits.

> ♠ K Q
> ♡ 5
> ◇ Q 10 8 7
> ♣ A K 9 7 5 2

Rebid 2NT despite the distribution. As we will see in a moment, responder has ways of discovering which suits are guarded.

3♣	A 6-card suit and not more than one outside guard.
3◇	Probably 4–6 in the minors and upper range.

> ♠ Q 5
> ♡ 4
> ◇ K J 8 4
> ♣ A J 10 8 4 2

This hand does not justify 3◇; rebid 3♣, treating it as a one-suiter with one outside guard.

> ♠ 7 4
> ♡ 3
> ◇ A K 9 2
> ♣ A Q J 9 8 3

Not lacking in 'class', rebid 3◇.

4♣	This is a rare rebid on a hand with strong playing values in clubs, e.g.

> ♠ 6
> ♡ A Q J
> ◇ 6 4
> ♣ A Q 10 9 7 5 3

We return now to the response of 2♢ itself. It fulfils three main purposes:

1. It is Staymanic, giving the partnership a chance to find a 4-4 fit in a major.

Responder holds:

> ♠ K J 8 5
> ♡ A 4
> ♢ 9 7 6 3
> ♣ J 4 2

He bids 2♢, as there could be a game in spades. If opener's rebid is 2♡ responder can transfer to 3♣, not forcing.

2. It allows time for development on all likely game hands.

Responder bids 2♢ with any of the following:

> ♠ A J 10 7 6 4
> ♡ 5 2
> ♢ A 6 3
> ♣ Q 2

This is too strong for the non-forcing 2♠ and the values are too widely dispersed for the jump to 3♠. Responder's best move is to bid 2♢ and introduce his spades on the next round.

> ♠ Q
> ♡ A 8 4
> ♢ K 9 7 3 2
> ♣ K 8 4 3

A jump to 5♣ would not be inappropriate on the values, but there is no need to hasten. Responder bids 2♢ to learn more about his partner's hand. If the rebid is 2♠ he must jump to 4♣, as 3♣ would not be forcing.

> ♠ A Q 8 6 3
> ♡ A K J 6 2
> ♢ 5
> ♣ Q 3

This could well be a slam hand, but time is needed to determine the best contract.

3. It enables the partnership to discover whether the necessary guards are held for 3NT.

There are two special sequences designed to check whether all suits are stopped for game in notrumps.

(a) 2♣–2◇–3♣–3◇. Here opener has shown a 6-card suit with only one guard outside clubs. Responder's second bid of 3◇ asks where the guard lies. Opener bids 3♡ or 3♠ with a guard in the suit named, 3NT with a guard in diamonds.

(b) 2♣–2◇–2NT–3◇. Now the opener has shown two guards outside clubs. Again, 3◇ asks where the guards lie. Opener bids 3♡ with hearts and diamonds, 3♠ with spades and diamonds, 3NT with both majors.

This example shows how a precision Pair avoids the ignominy of playing in 3NT with a suit wide open:

West	East
♠ K J 3	♠ Q 9 6 4
♡ 5	♡ Q 3
◇ A 8 2	◇ K J 4 2
♣ A Q 9 7 6 3	♣ K 8 2

The bidding goes:

West	East
2♣	2◇
2NT (1)	3◇ (2)
3♠ (3)	4♣ (4)
5♣ (5)	pass

(1) The rebid indicates simply that there are guards in two suits outside clubs.

(2) East makes a further relay bid of 3◇ to establish which suits are guarded.

(3) This rebid shows that the guards are in spades and diamonds.

(4) Knowing that the hearts are unprotected, East is prepared to settle for a part-score . . .

(5) . . . but West, with controls in four suits, is clearly worth a game bid.

The play

Against 5♣ the defence begins with two rounds of hearts. West ruffs and leads a club to the king, the standard safety play to take care of J 10 x x in the South hand. Assuming no trump loser, West needs only to bring down the ten of spades, or to find the spades 3–3, and if these chances fail there is still the diamond finesse. (Expert players will note that if North is left with the control in spades and has four diamonds there will be a 'show-up squeeze', enabling declarer to pick up South's doubleton queen of diamonds.)

When there is intervention over 2♣

Double of intervention at the two level is sputnik, the opener rebidding on natural lines. It follows that when the responder has the elements of a normal penalty double he should usually pass, and if the next player passes the opener should protect on any hand where it seems as though partner may have been lying in wait. The double is used on two types: when responder has moderate values and wants to compete, or when he is too strong for a non-forcing bid in a suit.

2NT over intervention is natural, with a guard in the enemy suit.

Any suit bid is natural and non-forcing. With a fair suit and game values responder doubles first and introduces his suit later.

A cue-bid occupies more bidding space than a sputnik double and its primary use is to request opener to bid 3NT with even a semi-guard in the opponent's suit. South opens 2♣, West overcalls with 2♠, and North holds:

(1) ♠ J 5 3
    ♡ A 8
    ◇ K J 6 3 2
    ♣ A 10 4

Bid 3♠, inviting partner to bid 3NT with A x in spades or even Q x.

(2) ♠ A 8 4
    ♡ A K 6 4 3
    ◇ 5 2
    ♣ J 10 5

Here responder has a choice between 3NT, which will go well if there are six club tricks to run, and 3♠, which will result in 3NT if opener has a bolster in spades, and otherwise in 5♣. The cue-bid is better because, if partner cannot respond 3NT, there will probably be a fair play for 5♣. You don't want to be in 3NT if partner has a singleton spade and the clubs are not solid.

$$(3) \quad
\begin{array}{l}
♠ \ 6\,4 \\
♡ \ A\,J\,8\,5 \\
◇ \ A\,10\,8\,2 \\
♣ \ K\,7\,5
\end{array}$$

Now a sputnik double is best, because responder needs to find opener with a fully-fledged guard in spades, not just a half-guard.

Summary

An opening bid of 2♣ is made on hands in the 12–15 range containing a 6-card suit with or without a side suit, or a 5-card suit and a 4-card major.

Responses: 2◇ relay (see below); 2♡ 2♠ 5-card suit, invitational; 2NT natural, 10–12; 3♣ constructive, not forcing; 3◇ strong suit, not forcing; 3♡ 3♠ inviting game in the suit; 4♣ 5♣ defensive raises.

Relay response of 2◇ is used on three main types: in search of a 4–4 fit in a major, to allow time for development on likely game hands, or to establish whether the necessary guards are held for 3NT.

Opener's rebid after 2♣–2◇. Opener shows a 4-card major; bids 2NT with six clubs and guards in two other suits; 3♣ with a 6-card suit and only one outside guard; 3◇ with 4–6 in the minors and good playing strength; 4♣ with strong playing values in clubs only. Over 2NT or 3♣ responder may bid 3◇ to inquire for guards.

After intervention at the two level double is sputnik and may be made either on moderate values where responder wishes to compete or on a strong hand where he intends later to introduce a 5-card suit; suit bids are natural and non-forcing; 2NT is natural; a cue-bid in the first instance asks opener to bid 3NT with a half-guard (Q x or J x x or better) in the opponent's suit.

15 OPENING 2♦

An opening 2♦ in the Precision system plays a specialized but important role. Consider these two hands:

	(1)	♠ A Q 7 3	(2)	♠ K J 8 4
		♡ K 9 5 4		♡ A K 10 6
		♢ 4		♢ —
		♣ K Q 5 3		♣ K 8 7 5 3

There is nothing you can open on either hand that does not violate one of the system's cherished principles. It is true that on hand (2) you could open 2♣, but the system of responses does not allow for this distribution.

The solution on both hands is to open 2♦. When Precision was in its youth the opening was used only on these particular distributions, 4-4-1-4 or 4-4-0-5, range 12 to 15. The bid received a degree of attention quite out of proportion to its value or frequency. In Britain we increased the frequency of the opening by extending it to 4-4-4-1 with the singleton in clubs; there was no problem in organizing the responses satisfactorily, but nothing much was gained, in terms of economy, because with 4-4-4-1 or 4-4-5-0 it is equally convenient to open 1♢.

The Americans then came up with a better idea: they decided to increase the work rate by opening 2♦ on hands with 3-4-1-5 or 4-3-1-5 distribution, such as:

	(3)	♠ K 10 8 4	(4)	♠ K J 2
		♡ A Q 3		♡ Q J 7 3
		♢ 4		♢ 6
		♣ A 7 6 4 2		♣ A K 8 5 3

One advantage of this procedure is that it removes a fairly large group of hands from the orbit of the tetchy 2♣ opening and gives them more accurate definition.

Players who have grappled with the Roman 2♦ opening will find the Precision 2♦ much easier to handle. This is because the shortage is already known. As we will see later, after the conventional response of 2NT the opener can define both his distribution and his range in a single bid.

(a) Responses on limited hands

On all weak hands the responder's first objective is to find a playable contract. West opens 2◇, North passes, and East holds:

$$(1) \quad \spadesuit \ J\,7\,4$$
$$\heartsuit \ 6\,3\,2$$
$$\diamondsuit \ Q\,8\,5\,2$$
$$\clubsuit \ 10\,4\,3$$

Respond 2♡ and hope the weather keeps fine. Opener will in no circumstances raise and if he has only three hearts he will transfer to 2♤. Here is an example of the sort of scrambling that takes place when the responder is weak:

West	East
♤ K Q 6 2	♤ 8 5
♡ A 10 3	♡ J 7 4
◇ 4	◇ Q 7 6 5 3
♧ K J 9 5 4	♧ 10 6 2

The bidding goes:

West	East
2◇ (1)	2♡
2♤ (2)	3♧ (3)
pass	

(1) When both openings are possible, prefer 2◇ to 2♧; it gives the partnership a better chance to settle in a playable contract at the two level.

(2) With only three hearts opener must never pass the 2♡ response.

(3) When 2♡ is removed, East knows that his partner must be 4–3–1–5.

On this occasion, as it happens, an opening 2♧ by West would have worked out better.

Again West has opened 2◇ and East holds:

$$(2) \quad \spadesuit \ Q\,6\,4$$
$$\heartsuit \ 6\,2$$
$$\diamondsuit \ J\,8\,5\,3$$
$$\clubsuit \ K\,8\,6\,2$$

Respond 3♣, which at least will be a 4–4 fit, and quite possibly a 5–4 fit. It is undesirable to respond 2♠ on a 3-card suit, for whereas a player with three hearts will always remove 2♡ to 2♠ he will always pass a response of 2♠.

(3)   ♠ 6 4
♡ Q 8 6
♢ K J 9 5 2
♣ 10 7 6

Respond 2♡ in preference to passing. If opener transfers to 2♠, showing 4–3–1–5 shape, bid 2NT.

(4)   ♠ 8 5 2
♡ 4
♢ Q 10 8 6 5 3
♣ J 7 2

Now it is advisable to pass. You might be better off in 2♠, but this could be a 3–3 'fit'.

(5)   ♠ Q 6 2
♡ J 4
♢ K 8 6 4 2
♣ 7 4 3

This 3–2–5–3 shape is awkward. The objection to 2♠ is that partner may hold only three, while 3♣ takes you a range higher on what may be a 4–3 fit. Still, 3♣ is probably the best answer; 5–4–3–1 is a much commoner shape than 4–4–4–1, so the odds are that partner has five clubs.

The only constructive response to 2♢ (apart from 2NT, which is forcing) is 3♢. This shows a strong suit and chances of game, probably in notrumps.

West	*East*
♠ 9	♠ A J 10 4
♡ A 10 5	♡ J 7 4 2
♢ A Q J 10 8 3	♢ 6
♣ J 4 2	♣ A K 7 3

With East the dealer, the bidding goes:

102

West	East
—	2♦
3♦ (1)	3♠ (2)
3NT	pass

(1) Inviting game unless partner has a void in diamonds or is otherwise unsuitable.

(2) Stressing the spade control and implying moderate hearts. If West had held a slightly different hand 5♦ might have been a better proposition than 3NT.

The play

If North draws the right inferences from the bidding and leads a heart against 3NT the contract may be in some jeopardy. If, as is more likely, North leads a spade through dummy's strength, declarer must go up with the ace and clear the diamonds. To play a low spade at trick one would give South the chance to win and make an astute lead such as the queen of hearts from Q x x, driving out the entry from the closed hand.

While it is possible to devise special meanings for responses of 3♥ or 3♠, their value would be so limited that it is better to dispense with them. As 2NT elucidates both distribution and range, there is no need for other intermediate responses.

A response of 3NT is natural, with a double guard in diamonds, obviously.

(b) Response of 2NT

When the responder sees chances of game but is uncertain about the best contract he seeks information with 2NT. The opener rebids according to the following schedule.

Opener's rebids after 2♦–2NT

3♣	3–4–1–5 and lower range. (It is usual in artificial sequences for clubs to be 'tied' to hearts, and here 3♣ signifies four hearts.)

3◇	4–3–1–5 and lower range. (Diamonds are 'tied' to spades.)
3♡	3–4–1–5 and upper range.
3♤	4–3–1–5 and upper range. Thus all rebids of three in a suit signify the semi-3-suiter type with five clubs and 4–3 or 3–4 in the majors.
3NT	4–4–1–4 and singleton king or ace of diamonds. This information will sometimes allow responder, with a diamond holding such as A x x or J 10 x x, to play in notrumps.
4♧	4–4–1–4 and lower range. It is assumed that as responder has bid 2NT he is prepared to play at game level in one or other major, having found a 4–4 fit.
4◇	4–4–0–5. (With a minimum it may be advisable to treat this hand as 4–4–1–4 and rebid 4♧.)
4♡	4–4–1–4 and upper range.

These sequences are easy to remember if one thinks of the logic behind them. 3♧ and 3◇ express the lower-range 5–4–3–1 types, leaving room to stop short of game, 3♡ and 3♤ the upper range of 5–4–3–1; 3NT reflects the bolster in diamonds – the singleton ace or king; 4♧ shows the lower range of 4–4–1–4 and 4♡ the upper range; finally, 4◇ marks the diamond void.

After the rebids of 3♧ and 3◇ the bidding may stop short of game. Here is an example:

West	East
♤ K J 7 3	♤ A 10 4
♡ A J 8	♡ K 9 6 2
◇ 5	◇ Q 8 7 3
♧ K 10 6 4 2	♧ Q 6

The bidding goes:

West	East
2◇	2NT
3◇ (1)	3♡ (2)
pass	

(1) Showing 4–3–1–5 distribution and lower range.

(2) The rebid is disappointing for East. At this stage 3♣ 3♡ or 4♣ would all be non-forcing. East chooses 3♡ because the diamond ruffs will be taken in the shorter trump hand. It is not an altogether happy contract, but as good as most systems would reach.

On this next hand the players are more fortunate in their search for a fit:

	West	East
♠	A 10 7 3	K J 9 4
♡	K 9 6 4	A J 5
◇	—	J 8 6 2
♣	A Q 10 6 2	K 4

The bidding goes:

West	East
2◇	2NT
4◇ (1)	6♠ (2)
pass	

(1) Showing 4–4–0–5 distribution and not a minimum.
(2) No need to go fishing after this highly encouraging rebid.

The play

Playing in 6♠, East ruffs the diamond lead and his best play at trick two is to run the ten of spades. If this loses and a trump is returned, East wins in hand, ruffs another diamond, returns to the king of clubs and draws the last trump (or trumps). There are numerous chances for the contract.

Guess what happened to East-West at one table when the deal above occurred in the European Championship. West opened 1♣ (natural), East made a learned approach with 1◇, and West bid 1♡; then came 2NT from East, 3NT from West. South led a diamond from A Q 10 x x x and East unhappily lost the first six tricks.

(c) When there is intervention over 2◆

A defender who has a strong hand will usually pass over 2◊ to see which way things are going. He expects to gain a better picture after the response.

When opponents do interfere, any bid by responder is natural, including double, or 2NT, or three of a suit. The only force is a cue-bid of the opponent's suit. This must be the right method because responder already has a good picture of his partner's hand. The bidding begins:

South	West	North	East
2◊	2♠	?	

North holds:

♠ 7 4
♡ K 10 6 3
◊ A 9 7 5 2
♣ Q 6

North competes with 3♡. If South has a minimum with only three hearts he is not obliged to continue.

Summary

The opening bid of 2◊ is made on 3-suiters or semi-3-suiters in the 12–15 range, with the shortage always in diamonds. The possible distributions are 3–4–1–5, 4–3–1–5, 4–4–1–4, and 4–4–0–5.

Responses: Pass suggests long diamonds and no fit for any other suit. 2♡ may be very weak with only three hearts; opener who has three hearts himself must transfer to 2♠. 2♠ and 3♣ are natural and limited, indicating a wish to play at this level. 2NT is forcing, see below. 3◊ is invitational, with a strong diamond suit.

Response of 2NT is made on hands with game chances where the final contract is uncertain. Opener rebids 3♣ with moderate, 3♡ with stronger 3–4–1–5; 3◊ with moderate, 3♠ with stronger 4–3–1–5; 3NT with 4–4–1–4 and singleton ace or king of diamonds; 4♣ with moderate, 4♡ with stronger 4–4–1–4; and 4◊ with fair 4–4–0–5.

When there is intervention over 2◊ all calls by third hand are natural. The only force is a cue-bid.

16 OPENING 2♥ AND 2♠

As 1♣ is the standard opening on strong hands, 2♥ and 2♠ are available for what are popularly known as 'weak two bids'. Psychologically, I think it is more sensible to regard them, not as mini-pre-empts, but as part of the constructive system.

Opening requirements

The requirements (open to variation in third and fourth position) are a strong 6-card suit and 7 to 10 points. We say '7 to 10' rather than '7 to 11' because most 11-point hands with a good major suit qualify for an opening bid of one.

Some players use weak two bids in the manner of a schoolboy throwing a lump of wood onto a railway track to see what will happen. Any hand with a long suit that is a king or so under an average opening tempts them to this aggressive display. They have their moments, but the bid often recoils.

One gets better results from maintaining a disciplined attitude. It is unwise to open a two bid on any hand that is too weak in playing tricks or too strong either in controls or distribution. These examples will show where the line should be drawn:

(1)   ♠ A J 7 6 4 2
        ♥ J 4
        ◇ 6 3
        ♣ J 7 5

The spades are sub-normal for a two bid, and as the hand is also minimum in other respects it is better to pass.

(2)   ♠ J 8 6 3
        ♥ A Q 10 6 4 2
        ◇ Q 3
        ♣ 5

Here the objection to 2♥ is that the hand would play well in the other major. It is generally undesirable, in first or second hand, to open a two bid on any hand that is capable of playing particularly well in a different strain – particularly the other major. This rules out most hands containing a void:

      (3) ♠ A 10 8 7 5 3
            ♡ —
            ♢ K 9 6 5 2
            ♣ Q 3

To open 2♠ as dealer 'to shut out the hearts' would be misguided for at least two reasons. Firstly, it is not so urgent to pre-empt when you hold a void of the suit you fear as when you hold two or three low cards; there is always the possibility that opponents will run into a bad break if you give them rope. Secondly, by opening 2♠ you are as likely to shut your own side out of five or six diamonds as to shut the opponents out of four hearts.

      (4) ♠ A 7
            ♡ J 10 8 6 5 3
            ♢ K J 9
            ♣ 4 3

To open 2♡ here would be questionable because the virtue of the hand lies outside the heart suit. In third or fourth hand, depending on the vulnerability, there would be a better case for trying to snatch a part score.

As I see it, the role of the two bid in Precision is to distinguish between an opening with normal defensive values and what used to be called an 'Acol opening', such as:

      (5) ♠ K J 10 8 7 4
            ♡ 4 2
            ♢ A J 5
            ♣ 6 3

By opening 2♠ you seize bidding space without giving a hostage to fortune, and you assist, instead of obstructing, your own side's chance of arriving at its best contract.

Length in the suit may compensate to a limited extent for lack of high cards. It is reasonable to open 2♠ on:

      (6) ♠ A 10 9 7 6 4 3
            ♡ 5
            ♢ Q 7 2
            ♣ 6 4

If the next player overcalls with 3♡ and your partner doubles, at least you will be contributing an ace. I wouldn't advise the opening if the spades were headed by K J 9 instead of by the ace. That is one of the differences between an opening two bid and an opening three bid: when you open a three bid you make no promise about defensive tricks, but a two bid is expected to contain a glint of steel.

System of responses

Although weak two bids have been played for many years there is no unanimity about the best system of responses. In the round robin stage of the 1972 world championship eleven of the eighteen pairs used weak two bids, yet there were no fewer than ten different systems of responding.

The only point on which there is general agreement is that a response of 2NT should be conventional and forcing. Opinions differ about the significance of a new suit at the three level. One scheme is to treat direct responses in a new suit as forcing; when responder wants to play in his suit at the three level he bids 2NT, opener is required to bid 3♣, and responder then introduces his suit. This strikes me as a singularly poor notion for three reasons: one is that, if 2NT is forcing, you can do without any other forcing response; a second, that there are very few hands where it is sensible for responder to seek to play in his own suit at a higher level; a third, that it is wasteful for the 2NT response to extract an automatic rebid of 3♣. The most useful function of 2NT is to obtain more information from the opener. We return to that later, but first, here is the general scheme of responses, which corresponds closely to modern American ideas.

Responses to 2♡ (or 2♠)

New suit Invites support for the suit, but limited. Respond 3◇ on:

$$♠ A62$$
$$♡ 4$$
$$◇ AQJ9643$$
$$♣ 64$$

On the same hand without the ace of spades, pass. You might or might not be better off in 3◇, but anyway you would be outgunned and happy to play in 2♡ undoubled.

2NT   Forcing, see below for full treatment.

Single raise   Defensive, ranging from a fair hand where there is a chance of making 3♡ and responder wants to discourage competition, to a rather weak hand where the aim is purely obstructive. Thus, raise to 3♡ on either

> ♠ Q 6
> ♡ A 10 8
> ◇ K 9 7 5 3 2
> ♣ J 6

or

> ♠ 8 6 4 3
> ♡ Q 8 7
> ◇ A 5 4 2
> ♣ 7 4

The opener never bids four over this raise.

Game raise   This, too, is an ambiguous call. It may be a bold pre-empt or it may be based on good values. The opponents have to guess at a high level.

3NT   To play, and perish the partner who insists on taking you back to his own suit!

The response of 2NT

As I mentioned above, there are different theories about the way in which the opener should rebid over this forcing response. The Italian method is for opener to rebid on a step system. Briefly, he bids 3♣ when in lower range of high cards and quality of suit, 3◇ with fair points but suit not so strong, 3♡ with low points and good suit (such as K Q J 9 x x upwards), 3♠ with good points and good suit. This is a playable system, though somewhat artificial.

The style recommended in previous books on Precision is for

opener to indicate a shortage with his rebid; with no singleton he rebids his suit when in lower range, bids 3NT when in upper range. This can be useful on occasions, but whereas singletons in the *short* trump hand are very important, in the *long* hand they are much less so. Furthermore, the responder gets no picture of the opener's range.

I feel it is more helpful for opener to give some picture (a) as to whether he is in upper or lower range, and (b) as to where his side values lie. Thus I prefer the style recommended by Howard Schenken, who was one of the first experts to adopt weak two bids. In his system an opener who is minimum rebids his suit and when not minimum shows a feature such as K J x or Q 10 x x in a side suit. Here are some examples of opener's rebids after 2♠–2NT:

(1)   ♠ A Q J 7 5 3
       ♡ 6 4
       ♢ J 5
       ♣ 7 3 2

Minimum, rebid 3♠.

(2)   ♠ K Q 10 8 7 4
       ♡ Q J
       ♢ Q 9 6 2
       ♣ 3

Upper range of high cards and spade suit adequate; rebid 3♢ showing the side feature. If partner then bids only 3♠ you are not obliged to bid four.

(3)   ♠ A K Q 10 6 4
       ♡ 7 5
       ♢ 10 8 7
       ♣ 7 2

Rebid 3NT, giving a picture of the more or less solid suit.

Showing the side feature over 2NT will sometimes help responder to judge whether the hands fit well, but more often he just wants to know the opener's range. Remember that a direct raise to three is not a game try, so when responder wants to invite game the only bid at his disposal is 2NT.

	West	East
♠	A 6	♠ K 7 4 3
♡	K 10 9 7 5 2	♡ 8 6 3
◇	7 6	◇ A Q J
♣	Q 10 5	♣ K 7 3

The bidding goes:

West	East
2♡	2NT
3♣ (1)	4♡ (2)
pass	

(1) Borderline, perhaps, as the trump suit is moderate, but it is normal to show the side feature unless definitely minimum. Bidding 3♣ does not commit the partnership to game.

(2) East would have passed a sign-off of 3♡ and over 3◇ would have bid only 3♡, as it would have looked as though the diamond honours were falling on top of one another. Over 3♣ he is able to take the final decision.

The play

North leads a low diamond against 4♡ and dummy's jack holds the trick. A trump is led from the table and South plays the four. Assuming that the diamond finesse is right, West can afford to lose two tricks in hearts and should finesse the nine. If this loses to the jack or queen he can return to dummy for the next heart lead. The play saves the contract when North has a singleton ace.

Reverting to the bidding of this hand, it is interesting to note how the use of a relay (2NT) increases the range of expression open to the partnership. Instead of East raising to three and West bidding or not bidding four, West is able to say, 'My opening was not a minimum and I have a feature in clubs', East can then either bid game or bid 3♡, saying 'I have made my effort, your bid doesn't excite me', and West can then pass or go on. The relay more than doubles the number of messages exchanged.

112

When there is intervention over 2♡ or 2♤

Over intervention, double is for penalties and suit bids are natural and non-forcing. A raise is competitive but not purely defensive, so opener is not barred from going on to game.

Summary

An opening 2♡ or 2♤ is made on a good 6-card or 7-card suit and 7 to 10 points. In first or second hand the opening should be restricted to hands that are not particularly suitable for any other strain.

Responses: Single raise is defensive. New suit is invitational. 2NT is forcing; opener who is minimum signs off in his suit; if not minimum he shows a side feature such as K J x; with a near-solid suit (A K Q x x x) he bids 3NT.

Over intervention double is for penalties, suit bids are natural and non-forcing, a raise may be competitive but is not purely defensive.

17 OPENING BIDS FROM 2NT TO 4♠

Openings from 2NT to 4♠ are grouped as follows:

    (a) Opening 2NT.
    (b) Opening 3♣.
    (c) Opening 3◇ 3♡ and 3♠.
    (d) Opening 3NT.
    (e) Opening 4♣ and 4◇.
    (f) Opening 4♡ and 4♠.

(a) Opening 2NT

There is not a lot to say about this opening, which shows a balanced 22–23 points, so this may be a convenient moment to review the notrump structure of the Precision system.

13 to 15	Open 1NT.
16 to 18	Open 1♣, rebid 1NT.
19 to 21	Open 1♣, rebid 2NT.
22 to 23	Open 2NT.
24 to 26	Open 1♣, rebid 3NT.

Most of the responses to 2NT are the same as after the sequence 1♣–1◇–2NT. A doubtful point, not of much importance, is whether to play 3◇ as natural or as a weak transfer to 3♡ (Flint convention, as described in Chapter 3). It seems to me that with a bad hand and a 5-card suit one might as well let partner play in 2NT; with a 6-card major it must be reasonable to try for game, so the convention cannot have much value opposite a 22–23 opening. On that basis, the schedule is as follows:

Responses to 2NT (22–23)

3♣	Baron, asking for 4-card suits 'upwards'. When the opener's only suit is clubs he rebids 3NT.
3◇	Natural, with aspirations beyond 3NT.
3♡ 3♠	Forcing. The sequence 2NT–3♡–3NT–4♡ carries a slam suggestion; 2NT–4♡ does not.

4♣ 4◇   Transfers to 4♡ and 4♠ respectively.

An alternative method is to use 3◇ as transfer to 3♡ (not necessarily weak) and treat 4♣ as Gerber, asking for aces. Opener bids 4◇ with 0 or 4 aces, 4♡ with 1, 4♠ with 2, 4NT with 3.

(b) Opening 3♣

Opening bids of 3♣ and 3◇ have not received much attention in previous accounts of the system. Goren's book contains no examples and appears to treat three of a minor as a pre-empt similar to three of a major. The summary by C. C. Wei describes the opening as a 'semi-solid 7-card minor, outside entry, invitational to 3NT'.

It is all right to play 3◇ as a pre-empt, as with a strong diamond hand (short of a 1♣ opening) one can begin with 1◇ and follow with 3◇. But how do you treat the following in Precision?

♠ A 4
♡ 6 5 3
◇ 7
♣ A K Q 8 7 5 3

You are some way short of a 1♣ opening and with eight playing tricks you are some way above a 2♣ opening. Nor does the hand qualify for an opening 3NT (see below).

Hands of this type – a strong club suit with one or two guards outside – are not so uncommon, and if you treat 3♣ as a pre-emptive opening you cannot portray them accurately in the system. As a pre-emptive 3♣ is nobody's idea of a nuclear weapon, it seems right to forgo the pre-empt and plug what would otherwise be a gap in the constructive scheme.

An opening 3♣, therefore, indicates the type on which, in a standard system, a player might open 1♣ and rebid 3♣. These are two examples:

(1) ♠ K J 7   (2) ♠ 8 4
    ♡ 5   ♡ K Q 6
    ◇ A 8   ◇ 7 2
    ♣ K Q J 9 7 6 3   ♣ A K Q J 9 5

The first hand contains two guards outside clubs, the second only one. As the bidding will usually move in the direction of 3NT, responses at the three level initially indicate *guards* rather than a playable suit. A commonsense exchange of information on this basis will establish whether the partnership has one suit completely unguarded. For example, the bidding begins:

(1) 3♣   3♦   (2) 3♣   3♦
    3♠   3♥

In the first sequence it is clear that opener has no guard in hearts; in the second it is clear that he has no guard in spades, as with spades and hearts he would be bidding 3NT at this point. Thus responder will know whether or not to try for game in notrumps.

The one tricky situation occurs when the opening bid is 3♣ and the response 3♥. Suppose that the opener holds:

(1) ♠ A 8   (2) ♠ 10 7
    ♥ 5   ♥ 6
    ♦ K 10 4   ♦ A Q
    ♣ K Q J 8 6 5 3   ♣ A Q J 10 7 4 2

With (1) it may seem natural to bid 3NT, as he holds guards in both the unbid suits. But then, what is he to bid on (2)? He holds diamonds, the critical suit, so doesn't want to exclude 3NT, but he doesn't know whether his partner has a guard in spades. The Italians treat 3♠ in this sequence as a 'denial bid' saying 'I control the diamonds but not the spades'. That idea works but is capable of being disremembered. A simpler scheme is to bid 3♠ on hand (1) where you hold both suits; partner will transfer to 3NT. On (2), where you hold diamonds only, you bid 3NT, and if responder does not hold the spades he must remove to 4♣.

There is one other problem arising from 3♣ to which we must give attention. Because of the lack of space, hands with a fair major suit present a difficulty. This is the scheme:

With a powerful suit and slam possibilities, jump to game.

♠ A 7 5
♥ A K Q 10 7 3
♦ K 4
♣ 8 2

Over 3♣ bid 4♡.

With a suit strong enough to play in game, but presenting no slam prospects, bid the suit and rebid it.

$$♠ \text{ A Q J } 10 \, 8 \, 4 \, 2$$
$$♡ \text{ K Q } 5$$
$$♢ \text{ } 4 \, 3$$
$$♣ \text{ } 2$$

Respond 3♠ and follow with 4♠.

When you want to find partner with modest support in a major, raise to 4♣, a bid scarcely needed in a natural sense. Opener is asked to name a major in which he holds three cards or, possibly, a doubleton honour. (The sequence is akin to 1NT–2♣–2♢–3♢, asking for a 3-card major, sometimes called the Weissberger convention.)

$$(1) \quad ♠ \text{ A Q } 8 \, 6 \, 4 \, 2$$
$$♡ \text{ } 8 \, 4 \, 2$$
$$♢ \text{ K } 5$$
$$♣ \text{ } 7 \, 3$$

Raise 3♣ to 4♣, conventionally asking partner to name a major in which he holds support. If opener bids 4♡ (or 4♢) you may follow with 4♠. With a singleton spade opener will revert to 5♣.

$$(2) \quad ♠ \text{ K Q } 8 \, 7 \, 4$$
$$♡ \text{ A K } 9 \, 6 \, 2$$
$$♢ \text{ } 6 \, 5$$
$$♣ \text{ Q}$$

Again, bid 4♣ in the hope that partner may be able to express support for one of your majors.

There is one more conventional response to 3♣. A response of 4♢ asks for a side ace, opener bidding 4NT with the ace of diamonds (so as not to carry the bidding beyond 5♣). This response is useful when responder has a big hand containing a void, e.g.

$$♠ \text{ A K } 6 \, 4$$
$$♡ \text{ K } 10 \, 8 \, 6 \, 3 \, 2$$
$$♢ \text{ —}$$
$$♣ \text{ Q } 8 \, 7$$

To repeat, these are the responses to 3♣:

3◇ 3♡ 3♠	Initially a guard; if repeated, a strong suit.
4♣	Requests opener to name a major in which he holds some support, x x x or Q x.
4◇	Asks opener to name an ace outside clubs (4NT with the ace of diamonds).
4♡ 4♠	Slam prospects in the suit named.

In proportion to its frequency, this opening receives rather complicated treatment. But you know how it is – if you leave a sequence in the air it crops up in an important match just when you can't afford a game swing. The Italians, I may add, have many more ramifications. After opener has shown a guard, responder can inquire the nature of the guard, whether there is a side singleton, almost the time of day.

(c) Opening 3♦ 3♥ and 3♠

It is possible to play 3◇ as a fairly strong opening, but with some differences from 3♣. As it would be impossible, in the space, to organize intelligent responses allowing for either one or two outside guards, there must be only one guard and the diamonds must be self-supporting, not less than A K J x x x. That is all right when it turns up, but on grounds of frequency (and familiarity) it is probably advisable to play 3◇ as a normal pre-empt. Opening bids of 3♡ and 3♠ are also the familiar kind, a 7-card suit with about six playing tricks when not vulnerable, slightly stronger when vulnerable.

(d) Opening 3NT

Precision uses the same style of 3NT opening as Acol, known in America as the 'gambling 3NT'. The requirements are a solid 7-card minor suit, with not more than a queen outside.

When responder can judge that 3NT is unmakable he may either pass, often the best 'defence' on a weak hand, or take out into 4♣. Opener will then transfer to 4◇ if his suit is diamonds.

4NT is a general slam try; opener is requested to bid six if he has an extra value such as a side queen or an eighth trump.

4◇ over 3NT is a conventional bid asking opener to name a singleton. Opener bids 4♡ or 4♤ with a singleton in that suit, 5♧ or 5◇ with a singleton in the opposite minor, 4NT when 7–2–2–2.

West	East
♤ A Q 8 5	♤ J 4
♡ A J 9	♡ 10
◇ A Q 6	◇ 8 4 2
♧ J 6 3	♧ A K Q 9 7 5 2

With East the dealer, the bidding goes:

West	East
—	3NT
4◇ (1)	4♡ (2)
6♧ (3)	pass

(1) West can count ten top tricks, with other chances, and asks first for partner's singleton. Over 4♤ he intends to make one more try with 4NT.

(2) Showing a singleton heart.

(3) This suits West quite well, especially as the lead in clubs will come up to his hand.

The play

North makes the safe lead of a club against 6♧, played by West. The king is played from dummy and South follows suit. The jack of spades is covered by the king and ace. Now the contract is guaranteed, barring a ruff of the next spade. Declarer cashes the queen of spades, ruffs a low spade with a high trump, returns to the jack of clubs, and ruffs the last spade. Then he leads the ten of hearts from dummy and plays low unless South covers (in which case the J 9 will be equals and two diamonds can be discarded). When North wins the trick he must lead back into the A Q of diamonds or A J of hearts.

(e) Opening 4♣ and 4♦

These are 'Texas' openings, requesting opener to transfer to 4♡ and 4♤ respectively. They are stronger than a pre-emptive opening of 4♡ or 4♠. As a rough guide, they should contain the defensive values of an opening one bid in addition to a suit good enough for a pre-empt at the four level.

$$(1) \quad \begin{array}{l} \spadesuit \ A \ Q \ J \ 8 \ 7 \ 4 \ 3 \ 2 \\ \heartsuit \ K \ 9 \\ \diamondsuit \ Q \ 6 \\ \clubsuit \ 4 \end{array}$$

Open 4◇. This hand is in the lower range in respect of high cards.

$$(2) \quad \begin{array}{l} \spadesuit \ 4 \\ \heartsuit \ A \ K \ Q \ 9 \ 6 \ 4 \ 3 \\ \diamondsuit \ A \ 6 \ 3 \\ \clubsuit \ 7 \ 2 \end{array}$$

Open 4♣.

These Texas openings have three advantages, easily compensating for the loss of a natural pre-empt in clubs or diamonds:

1. They enable opener to make a distinction between a pre-emptive and a strong bid.

2. As a result of the transfer, nothing is known about the closed hand, which makes the defence more difficult.

3. Responder can propose a slam without going beyond game level. A bid of the intermediate suit, 4◇ over 4♣, 4♡ over 4◇, is a general slam suggestion without reference to the suit named. On hand (1) above opener would decline the invitation; on hand (2) he would accept it.

(f) Opening 4♥ and 4♠

These are normal pre-empts, limited as to range by the failure to open 4♣ or 4◇.

Summary

(a) **Opening 2NT** shows a balanced 22–23. Responses: 3♣ Baron; 3◇ natural; 3♡ 3♠ forcing; 4♣ 4◇ transfers to 4♡ and 4♠ respectively. The sequence 2NT–3♡–3NT–4♡ carries a slam suggestion.

(b) **Opening 3♣** indicates a strong suit with one or two outside guards. Responses: 3◇ 3♡ 3♠ initially a guard for notrumps,

4♣ requests opener to show modest support for a major; 4◇ asks for an ace outside clubs, opener rebidding 4NT with ace of diamonds; 4♡ 4♠ slam chances. After the sequence 3♣–3♡ opener with a guard in diamonds but not spades bids 3NT; with a guard in both he bids 3♠, for responder to transfer to 3NT.

(c) **Opening 3◇ 3♡ and 3♠** are normal pre-empts.

(d) **Opening 3NT** signifies a solid 7-card minor with at most a queen outside. Responses: 4♣ means 'unable to stand 3NT'; 4◇ asks for singleton, opener bidding 4♡ or 4♠ with singleton in that suit, 5♣ or 5◇ with singleton in the opposite minor, 4NT with 7–2–2–2; 4NT is a general slam try.

(e) **Opening 4♣ and 4◇** are 'Texas', requesting transfer to 4♡ and 4♠ respectively. They are stronger than a direct 4♡ or 4♠. A bid of the intermediate suit by responder is a slam suggestion.

(f) **Opening 4♡ and 4♠** are normal pre-empts.

121

18 DEFENSIVE AND COMPETITIVE BIDDING

Precision has not blazed any new trails in defensive bidding, though C. C. Wei has pointed out that an analogy may be observed between opening bids and defensive overcalls. A simple overcall at the one level is comparable to an opening bid of one; a jump overcall (American style) is equivalent to a weak two bid; and a take-out double corresponds to the opening 1♣.

As one of the objects of this book is to assist two players to form a first-class partnership, it is necessary to comment on certain disputed areas of defensive bidding. I propose also to describe some conventional bids that are common among tournament players and are surely worth adopting.

There is nothing new to say about simple overcalls, so these are the subjects I shall be covering:

> (a) Defence against 1NT.
> (b) Jump overcalls.
> (c) Michaels-type overcalls.
> (d) Defence to pre-empts.
> (e) Unassuming cue-bids.
> (f) Competitive doubles.

(a) Defence against 1NT

As more and more players use a weak notrump in all positions, the defence to 1NT has become an area of increasing importance. There are already many well known counter-measures: in the *Landy* convention an overcall of 2♣ signifies at least 5–4 in the majors; *Ripstra* bids 2♣ to indicate defence in clubs and both majors, 2♦ with diamonds and both majors; *Sharples* extends the range by bidding 2♣ with clubs and any two suits, 2♦ as above; *Astro* (similarly *Aspro*) bids 2♣ with hearts and another suit 2♦ with spades and another suit; *Goren's* book on Precision proposes 2♣ with a minor 2-suiter, 2♦ with a major 2-suiter in the Italian *Blue Club* all suit overcalls are Texas, asking for transfer to the suit above.

It is important to consider the main *tactical* objective when overcalling 1NT. Are you trying to find a sound contract of your own, or are you trying to push them out of 1NT?

At one time I espoused the *Aspro* method, which is designed for launching 2-suiters. I have now come round to the view that the most important task of any defensive scheme is to dislodge the opponents from 1NT (or to interfere with their Stayman manoeuvres). Thus the test of a good method is how often it enables the defenders to compete with reasonable safety. The defence when 1NT has been followed by three passes is tricky; opponents playing in 1NT too often get a good result, whether they make it or not.

By this test of flexibility, the best single weapon is an overcall of 2♣ to indicate that you are playable in clubs and two other suits. You may hold any variation of 4-4-4-1 or 5-4-3-1 or 5-4-4-0 so long as the short suit is not clubs. This is an example of how, with moderate values, you unseat the enemy from 1NT and scramble your way into a playable contract:

	West		East
♠	K 10 7	♠	Q 9 6 4 2
♡	K 9 6 3 2	♡	8 5
◇	4	◇	K 8 7 4
♣	A J 5 3	♣	9 7

With neither side vulnerable South opens 1NT and West overcalls with 2♣. East responds 2◇ (not 2♠, as this might be West's short suit). West transfers to 2♡, indicating that he cannot stand diamonds, and now it is safe for East to bid 2♠.

In response to this 2♣ overcall, 2NT is the only force. The player with the 3-suiter should now bid his lowest 4-card suit.

It is not entirely satisfactory to use an overcall of 2◇ in the same sense, as a 3-suiter showing diamonds, hearts and spades. In the first place the opportunities are rare; secondly, it means that you have no suitable overcall when you are 5-5-2-1 or 5-4-2-2 with both majors. It is better, therefore, to use 2◇ as equivalent to the Landy 2♣, promising at least 5-4 in the majors. In response, 2NT is natural; 3◇ is forcing and asks for the better major.

The combination I have proposed – Sharples 2♣ and Landy-type 2♦ – is known in the British tournament world as 'Cansino'.

A double of a weak notrump is in principle a penalty double and responder should rarely take it out. Some players maintain that the fourth player should leave in the double with a balanced Yarborough, but personally I regard that as a somewhat austere doctrine.

As players know from experience, there is seldom any advantage in doubling a strong notrump, and a double by a passed hand can never be sound. There is therefore a good case for attaching a special meaning to a double in these circumstances. The double now indicates either a major or a minor 2-suiter. Responder bids his better minor or a self-supporting major.

	West		East
♠	K Q 7 5 3	♠	10 8 6
♡	A Q 10 5 2	♡	4 3
♦	8	♦	A 9 6 5 2
♣	Q 4	♣	8 6 3

South opens a strong notrump and West, with a major 2-suiter, doubles. East responds 2♦, West transfers to 2♡, and East bids 2♠.

When a double would show a 2-suiter, 2♦, in the sense described above, becomes redundant. It is used instead in the Ripstra sense, to indicate a 3-suiter with diamonds, hearts and spades. The defensive scheme is therefore in two parts:

Action over a weak notrump by second or fourth, but not by a passed hand:

Double	In principle for penalties.
2♣	Playable in clubs and two other suits.
2♦	At least 5–4 in the majors.
2♡ 2♠	Natural.
2NT	Any pronounced 2-suiter other than a major 2-suiter.

Action over a strong notrump, or by a passed hand over any notrump:

Double	Either a major or a minor 2-suiter.
2♣	As above.
2♦	Playable in diamonds, hearts and spades.
2♡ 2♠	Natural.
2NT	Any pronounced 2-suiter not expressed by a double.

It is unprofitable to lay down any range for the conventional overcalls, as much depends on the vulnerability, type of scoring, quality of suits, and position at the table. As it is normal to double a weak notrump on about 15 upwards, the overcalls of 2♣ and 2♦ will generally fall between about 10 and 14. I certainly advise keeping the double up to strength. Nothing is more exasperating, in a team-of-four match, than to play like a tiger to record 120 or 150 and find that at the other table your teammates have conceded 380 for 1NT doubled and made with an overtrick.

(b) Jump overcalls

British players are accustomed to using quite strong jump overcalls: over an opponent's 1♦ they would bid 2♠ on A K J 9 x x and a side ace. Americans use the jump overcall as a pre-emptive weapon, ranging from A Q J 10 x x and a blank hand to as little as Q J 10 8 x x and 6–4–2–1 distribution.

One objection to weak jump overcalls is that the defender is committed to a take-out double on hands with poor preparedness for the other major. For example, 1♦ is opened on your right and you hold:

♠ 5
♡ A Q J 9 7 5
♦ 6 3 2
♣ A K 8

This is very strong, obviously, for a simple overcall. If you double there is a danger, it seems to me, that partner may leap to the sky in spades, especially if the opener's partner is able to 'bounce'.

Perhaps it doesn't often happen like that. Still, it leaves a gap in the defensive system not to have a bid for hands of this strength. The problem also arises with a strong minor suit; 1♡ on your right and you hold:

$$\spadesuit\ 6\ 4$$
$$\heartsuit\ 6\ 3$$
$$\diamondsuit\ A\ K\ Q\ 8\ 7\ 5\ 3$$
$$\clubsuit\ A\ 3$$

You want to invite 3NT, and if 3◇ is not a strong call you are really stymied.

As I remarked when discussing the 3♣ opening, I think it is right to tie up one's own end of the bidding before devising measures (pretty poor ones at that) to obstruct the opponents. So I recommend what may be described as 'intermediate' jump overcalls. Partner is expected to treat them seriously, though sometimes they may be under strength. For example, if partner has passed and an opponent opens 1◇ there is no harm in over-calling 2♠ on ♠A J 10 9 x x ♡x ◇K x x x ♣x x.

When the responder to a jump overcall has enough for game provided the overcaller is up to strength, he can allow lee-way by cue-bidding the enemy suit. With North-South vulnerable the bidding begins:

South	West	North	East
1◇	2♠	pass	?

East holds:

(1)   ♠ Q 4
      ♡ J 5 4
      ◇ 9 7 3 2
      ♣ A J 6 5

He is worth 3♠, a normal game try.

(2)   ♠ J 6
      ♡ A 10 7 3
      ◇ 7 6 4 2
      ♣ K J 3

Now he has the values for a raise to 4♠, but it may be advisable to hold back a little in case partner is 'at it'. Bid 3◇, saying 'I am worth 4♠, but I am giving you a chance to sign off in 3♠'.

(c) Michaels-type overcalls

Most tournament players have abandoned the ponderous cue-bids of the Culbertson era. There are many alternative schemes for overcalls in the opponent's suit and I propose a variation along the lines of the *Michaels* convention.

2♣ over 1♣, and 2♦ over 1♦, signify defence in both majors, normal range about 7 to 11, e.g.

	(1)	♠ K 10 8 6 3	(2)	♠ A Q 8 5
		♡ A J 6 4 2		♡ J 8 7 4 2
		♦ 6 3		♦ Q 5 2
		♣ 5		♣ 4

Both hands are suitable for a cue-bid over an opponent's minor-suit opening.

2♡ over 1♡ indicates a hand below the standard of a take-out double but containing five spades, e.g.

$$\begin{array}{l} ♠ \text{ Q 9 7 4 3} \\ ♡ \text{ 6} \\ ♦ \text{ A J 8 5} \\ ♣ \text{ K 6 2} \end{array}$$

Here there is a difference from the American convention, which demands a 5-card minor in addition to five spades.

2♠ over 1♠ promises five hearts and a 5-card minor, e.g.

$$\begin{array}{l} ♠ \text{ 6} \\ ♡ \text{ A Q J 7 4} \\ ♦ \text{ 4 2} \\ ♣ \text{ K Q 8 6 3} \end{array}$$

In response, 2NT asks the overcaller to name his minor suit. These distributional overcalls have the same sense in fourth and when the opening bid has been followed by two passes. They may also be used when both opponents have bid, in a sequence such as:

South	West	North	East
1♠	pass	1NT	2♠

Here East will have a hand of this type:

♠ 6
♡ A K 8 6 3
♢ K J 9 7 5 2
♣ 4

Precision also uses the well known 'unusual notrump', denoting length in both minors or in the two lowest unbid suits. Thus 2NT over an opening 1♢ indicates hearts and clubs, over 1♣ hearts and diamonds.

(d) Defence over pre-empts

It is usual nowadays to play double for take-out in all positions (that is to say, in second or fourth, over three of a major or three of a minor). In the British Precision team we lay stress on major-suit preparedness. The most awkward hands are the 5-4-2-2 types where there is support for only one major. For example, South opens 3♢ and West holds:

♠ K 5
♡ A K 10 5
♢ 6 2
♣ A Q 8 6 4

We prefer 3♡ to a double. It follows that responder should make free use of the cue-bid, giving the overcaller a chance to rebid a good suit or move to a better suit. In a competitive sequence the responder should incline to a double rather than a raise on moderate trumps.

A double of an opening 4♣ or 4♢ (natural, not Texas) implies quick tricks rather than trump strength. A double of 4♡ should contain tolerance for spades.

(e) Unassuming cue-bids

This is one of the most important advances in defensive tactics. During part-score competition a cue-bid by a defender whose partner has made a simple overcall denotes at first a sound, as opposed to a competitive, raise. The bidding begins:

South	West	North	East
1♦	1♠	2♣	?

East holds:

(1)	♠ K 9 5 3	(2)	♠ K 8 4
	♡ J 7		♡ A 10 8 6
	♦ 10 8 5 3		♦ 7 3
	♣ K 6 2		♣ Q 10 8 4

On the first hand he raises to 2♠, on the second he bids 2♦, which says initially, 'I have a sound raise to 2♠ with fair defensive values.'

The same distinction is made at the three level. A direct raise to three is pre-emptive, not inviting game; with all-round values the responder cue-bids and then raises to three.

The player who has made the simple overcall treats the cue-bid as equivalent to a sound raise. With a minimum he repeats his suit at the lowest level, with a fairly strong overcall he makes a constructive rebid.

These manoeuvres enable the defending side to compete with much more confidence and accuracy than is otherwise possible. Everyone knows this type of situation:

South	West	North	East
1♡	1♠	2♡	3♠
4♡	dble	pass	?

East holds:

♠ Q J 7 5
♡ 4
♦ K J 10 7 5
♣ 6 5 3

He has an awkward decision whether or not to stand the double. If he takes it out he may find that partner has K Q 10 of hearts and a singleton ace of diamonds. Playing unassuming cue-bids, East does not have to worry: he has already given the message that he is not strong defensively.

(f) Competitive doubles

There are many situations in the part-score area where doubles can be put to better use than to exact a penalty. These are the two most important:

1. When the defenders have supported one another at the two level, a double by the opening side is competitive, not for penalties.

South	West	North	East
1◇	1♡	1♠	2♡
dble			

The double is forward-going, South holding about 15 points and a doubleton spade, e.g.

> ♠ K 4
> ♡ 10 7 2
> ◇ A K 7 4 3
> ♣ A J 4

Suppose, next, that South had passed and North had doubled:

South	West	North	East
1◇	1♡	1♠	2♡
pass	pass	dble	

This, again, is competitive, North holding a hand of this type:

> ♠ A 9 5 4 2
> ♡ 7 4
> ◇ A 6
> ♣ Q 9 3 2

He does not want to lie down to 2♡ but has no suitable call other than the competitive double, which leaves several possibilities open.

2. The second occasion for a competitive double is when both sides have bid only one suit and there is no space for a trial bid at the three level.

South	West	North	East
1♡	2◇	2♡	3◇
dble			

The double invites game in hearts; it follows that 3♡ at this point would simply contest the part score. The double at this level is competitive, remember, only when each side has mentioned only one suit.

Summary

(a) **Defence to 1NT.** Overcall of 2♣ means playable in clubs and two other suits; the only forcing response to this is 2NT; the overcaller then names his lowest 4-card suit. Overcall of 2◊ (apart from the exception given below) signifies at least 5–4 in the majors; in response, 2NT is natural, 3◊ asks for the better major. Double of a weak notrump, or double by a passed hand, indicates either a major or a minor 2-suiter; in that situation 2◊ means playable in diamonds, hearts and spades.

(b). **Jump overcalls.** These are 'intermediate', ranging from strong to medium according to the tactical situation. Responder who is barely worth a raise to game may cue-bid the opponent's suit to allow the overcaller a chance to sign off.

(c) **Michaels-type overcalls.** 2♣ over 1♣, and 2◊ over 1◊, show at least 5–4 in the majors, range about 7 to 11. 2♡ over 1♡ indicates a hand below the standard of a take-out double but containing five spades. 2♠ over 1♠ promises five hearts and a 5-card minor; in response, 2NT asks for the minor.

(d) **Defence to pre-empts.** Double of a three bid is for take-out in all positions, always with major-suit preparedness.

(e) **Unassuming cue-bids.** During part-score competition a cue-bid by a defender whose partner has made a simple overcall denotes initially a sound, as opposed to a competitive, raise.

(f) **Competitive doubles.** When the defenders have supported one another at the two level, a double by the opening side is competitive. A double at the three level is competitive when each side has bid only one suit and there is no space for a trial bid.

Note. Competitive doubles (also unassuming cue-bids) are discussed at greater length in *Bridge for Tournament Players*, by Albert Dormer and myself.

19 SLAM CONVENTIONS

Apart from the asking bids described in the next chapter, Precision has not originated any new conventions for slam bidding, and I do not propose to suggest any here. However, it is necessary to have an understanding about the precise significance of cue-bidding, 4NT, 5NT, and five of a major.

(a) Cue-bidding

By an unfortunate piece of nomenclature, the term 'cue-bid' has three uses. It describes the immediate overcall of an opponent's suit; the bid of an opponent's suit in a competitive auction; and the promise of a control during a constructive auction. We are concerned here only with this third meaning.

A cue-bid occurs only when the trump suit has been agreed by a raise (or has been determined by a jump of some sort) and the partnership appears to be on the way to a slam. In a sequence such as 1♠–2♠–3◇, 3◇ is a trial bid, proposing game in spades; 1♠–2◇–3◇–3♡ might be a genuine suit or a notrump probe; but 1♠–3♠–4◇ would show a control, as the players are already committed to game.

The first cue-bid in any auction says four things: 'It is worth investigating a slam; I have first or second round control of the suit I am calling; this is my cheapest control (apart from suits already mentioned); I want to hear about your controls'.

Take this sequence:

West	East
1♠	2♡
3♡	4◇

Hearts are the agreed suit, at any rate for the present. East's 4◇ conveys the four messages outlined above: slam chances; control in diamonds; no control in clubs (which would have been a cheaper suit to mention); can you co-operate?'

At this point any bid by West above the level of 4♡ would be a slam acceptance and would logically imply control of clubs, even if clubs were not specifically mentioned. For example, 4♠ would suggest ace of spades and first or second round control of clubs. 4NT or 5♣, on the other hand, would tend to deny the ace of spades.

Four of a major is usually a playable contract

An important point of theory arises from the example above: when is four of a major a playable contract as opposed to a cue-bid?

The answer is that, unless there are definite indications to the contrary, four of a major suggests a playable contract and is not part of the chain of cue-bids. Suppose that the sequence above had continued in this fashion:

West	East
1♠	2♡
3♡	4◇
4♠	

Having chosen to bid 3♡ over 2♡, West could not logically want to play in 4♠, excluding 4♡. So 4♠ is a cue-bid and an exception to the general principle. But observe these more common examples:

(1)	West	East
	1♠	2◇
	3◇	4♣
	4♡	4♠

East's 4♣ was ostensibly a cue-bid with diamonds as the agreed suit, and West's 4♡ was an acceptance on that basis. But when East reverts to his partner's original suit, a different interpretation must be placed on his manoeuvres: he was intending to support spades all along, and his 4♣ was an advance cue-bid, designed to express his good support for spades. His bidding suggests something like ♠ A J x ♡ x x ◇ A Q x x ♣ K Q x x.

(2)	West	East
	1♠	2♡
	3♣	4♣
	4◇	4♡ or 4♠

Here West has made a cue-bid on the basis that clubs are the agreed suit, but East, whether he bids 4♡ or 4♠, is holding back and suggesting that it may be unwise to proceed beyond four of a major.

It is true that there are occasions when one would like to cue-bid in partner's major suit, but it is impossible to devise a rule that will serve on all occasions. It is better to have a general principle and stick to it. Otherwise you get the situation where one player cue-bids a void in his partner's major suit and the other player, reading this bid as delayed support, passes on K J x x x.

How to distinguish between kings and aces?

Below the game level, at least, no distinction is made between the four types of control – ace, void, king, singleton. In many cases one has the feeeling that the singleton will be critical and what partner wants to know about. For example, West holds:

♠ A Q J 7 4
♡ A K 8 5 2
◇ 4
♣ J 3

The bidding begins:

West	East
1♠	2♣
2♡	3♠
?	

West has a maximum one bid, and although his partner's 3♠ was limited he is entitled to make a forward move now. The bid most likely to inform and interest partner is 4◇.

The singleton is often mentioned in the way of an advanced cue-bid. West holds:

♠ A J 7 3
♡ Q 4
◇ A K 8 6 4 2
♣ 7

After 1◇–1♡–1♠–3♡ he should bid 4♣. As he would not be introducing a new suit at this point, 4♣ must be a cue-bid agreeing hearts.

134

However, the question arises, when kings singletons and aces are treated in the same way, is there not a danger of arriving at six with two aces missing?

The Italians, who have laid down the pattern for the modern style of cue-bidding, are a trifle bland about this. It can happen, they say, implying that it is part of growing up, like being arrested on Boat-race night.

However, there are one or two safety devices. When a player by-passes a suit and then bids it later, the presumption is that he lacks first-round control of this suit. The bidding goes:

West	East
1♡	2♢
3♢	4♧
4♢	<u>4♠</u>

Here East evidently has a control in spades, yet he by-passed that suit when he bid 4♧ over 3♢. The inference to be drawn is that he has first-round control of clubs, second-round control of spades.

A second safeguard is that the player who is making the running, as it were, should cue-bid only first-round controls when the bidding has passed game level. With no more aces to mention, he should adopt some other form of advance, such as a non-conventional 4NT.

The principle of subordination

In the last paragraph I used the phrase 'who is making the running'. That brings us to another aspect of cue-bidding. In most cases one of the partners initiates the action and the other follows him. The player in the subordinate role is expected to show his controls even if he has nothing in reserve, so long as he does not raise the level of the bidding. Here is a simple example; West holds:

♠ A Q 10 7 3
♡ J 9 5
♢ K Q 3
♧ 8 2

The bidding begins:

West	East
1♠	2♡
3♡	4♣
?	

West may reflect that his K Q of diamonds are part of his bid; nevertheless, it is his duty to bid 4◇, as this does not carry the bidding above four hearts. In the present case it is possible that all East wants to know is whether there are two losing diamonds; it is not West's business to speculate.

Thus there is a technique in cue-bidding, as in most things. Remember the main points: when, on the evidence, four of major might be a cue-bid, might be a playable contract, it should be assumed to be a playable contract; it is usual to show the cheapest control, and when the order is reversed the inference is that only second-round control is held in the suit that has been by-passed; and the subordinate player has a duty to show any control that does not take the partnership beyond the lowest game contract.

(b) Use of 4NT

A season of playing the Blue Club convinced me of one point very strongly: that the system's treatment of 4NT, and of the Blackwood convention, is far superior to the traditional method which simply distinguishes between quantitative and conventional.

The noteworthy feature of their method is that Blackwood is conventional only in two circumstances: when it occurs during the first two rounds (that is to say, as one of the first four bids made by the partnership) or when there is a jump. Thus

	(1)	1♠	2♡	or	(2)	1♠	2♣
		4♡	4NT			2◇	2♡
						3♣	4NT

are conventional, but

	(3)	1♡	1♠
		3♠	4◇
		4NT	

136

is not, even though a suit has been clearly agreed. 4NT in this case is what they call a 'general cue-bid', better rendered in English as 'general try'. It would mean here that the player wanted more information from his partner, probably an extra control of some sort.

The Blue Club uses a quantitative 4NT, or a natural 4NT when no suit has been agreed, in just the same way as Acol, but this 'general try' is something different. Believe me, it is a great relief to be able to make a general slam suggestion with 4NT and get a sensible and informative reply. You will find that you will use 4NT in this sense far more often than as an inquiry for aces.

Five-ace Blackwood

In the Italian scheme of responses to conventional Blackwood, 5◇ is the sign off showing no ace, and 5♣ shows one ace or four. There may be some logic in that arrangement – when no ace is held the bidding usually ends without further exploration—but I would not think of recommending such a reversal of normal practice. There is, however, obvious merit in the scheme known as five-ace Blackwood, in which the system of responses is as follows:

5♣	0 or 3 aces
5◇	1 or 4 aces
5♡	2 aces
5♠	2 aces and the king of a suit bid by the partnership
5NT	2 aces and 2 such kings

'A suit bid by the partnership' means, of course, a critical suit, such as the trump suit or main side suit. The bids at this level are as valuable in their negative as in their positive aspects.

Four types of Blackwood

To sum up, then, Blackwood may be of four types:

1. **Quantitative,** when a bid of notrumps is raised.
2. **Natural,** when a slam search has proved abortive and the player who bids 4NT has nothing more to say.

3. General try, forcing and asking for additional features; lacking any such feature, the responder must sign off in the trump suit.

4. Conventional, only when bid on the first or second round or with a jump; responses according to the five-ace schedule.

(c) Use of 5NT

The first bid to strike out is 5NT as a continuation of 4NT, asking for kings. That was always a silly notion. Except on rare occasions when it may be construed as natural, or as a general try for seven with no suit agreed, 5NT is best played as a trump asking bid, with responses as follows:

When the agreed suit is spades or hearts

6♣	No top honour
6♢	queen
6♡	king or ace
6♠	2 honours or K x x x x
6NT	3 top honours

If you find mnemonics helpful, I suggest the invented word OQUAT, standing for O, Q, K, A, Two.

When the agreed suit is diamonds

6♣	0 or queen

Then same progression as before.

When clubs is the agreed suit

6♣	0 or 1 top honour
6♢	2 top honours
6♡	3 top honours

The same mnemonic as before will stand for diamonds, so long as it is remembered that the first two responses are telescoped. For clubs, the mnemonic is simply 123.

(d) Five of a major

An advance to five of a major has one of two conventional meanings, depending on whether the player who makes the advance was first to bid the suit or is supporting his partner. This is the first situation:

West	East
1♠	2♡
3♢	4♠
5♠	

West, who first mentioned spades, bids five over four, spurning 4NT (general try) or a cue-bid in clubs. The inference to be drawn is that his trump suit is poor; he is not worried about side controls.

The message is different when the player who bids five is not the one who introduced the suit, as in this type of sequence:

West	East
1♡	1♠
3♡	5♡

The raise to 5♡ suggests that East has good cards in hearts and spades but no control in the unbid suits.

To repeat, a voluntary advance to five by a player who has bid a suit suggests that he is worried about the trump suit itself; a raise to five by the other player means that he has no extra control in an unbid suit.

Summary

(a) **Cue-bidding.** To avoid ambiguity, when four of a major might be a playable contract it is assumed to be this and not a cue-bid. A player making a cue-bid normally shows his cheapest control, and when he is seen to reverse this order it means that he lacks first-round control of the suit he has by-passed. A player whose partner has made the first cue-bid should not fail to show a control that does not raise the level of the bidding beyond the point of the lowest sign-off.

(b) **Use of 4NT.** A bid of 4NT may be either (1) a quantitative raise of partner's notrump bid, (2) a sign-off when no suit has been agreed and slam prospects seem dubious, (3) a 'general try', asking for additional features, or (4) conventional Blackwood only if made on the first two rounds or with a jump. The responses to conventional Blackwood are 5♣ 0 or 3, 5◇ 1 or 4, 5♡ 2, 5♠ 2 and a critical king, 5NT 2 and 2 critical kings.

(c) Use of 5NT. Generally a trump asking bid, with the following responses: suit hearts or spades, 6♣ 0, 6◇ queen, 6♡ king or ace, 6♠ 2 or K x x x x, 6NT 3 (mnemonic OQUAT); suit diamonds, 6♣ 0 or queen, then same progression; suit clubs, 6♣ 1, 6◇ 2 or K x x x x, 6♡ 3.

(d) Five of a major. By the player who first bid the suit, indicates worry about the trump suit; by his partner, means slam chances but no additional control in an unbid suit.

20 ITALIAN-STYLE ASKING BIDS

Asking bids are not a necessary part of the system. But they are fun, and they confer an advantage in a small but important area. It takes time to understand and play them, but once mastered they make the game easier. The scheme that follows is based on the ideas of Garozzo and Belladonna; but we (the British Precision players, that is) have trimmed the edges so that some simplifying rules can be laid down.

Outline of the method

Asking bids (in the scheme described here) occur only after a 1♣ opening and a positive response. At this stage the level of the bidding is low and there is room for detailed inquiry.

After 1♣ and a positive response *all* rebids by the opener except 2NT are asking bids of one kind or another. There are, in fact, three kinds:

Alpha, where the player who makes the asking bid introduces a new suit; his partner's response is tied to his holding in this suit and also has a bearing on his controls.

Beta, which is an inquiry for controls and takes place mostly after 1♣–1NT. (When asking bids are played, the range of 1NT is extended.) There is also Beta 4♣, again concerned with controls and asking for more definition.

Gamma, where the 1♣ bidder supports his partner's suit and asks for details of partner's holding in the suit.

The Alpha bid

Whenever the 1♣ opener bids a suit of his own after a positive response (apart from the sequence 1♣–1NT–2♣, which is another form of inquiry), he asks about partner's holding in this suit; at the same time partner gives information about his controls. Suppose the bidding begins 1♣–1♡–1♠; 1♠ is Alpha and asks for responses as follows:

1st step (1NT) No positive support for spades (less than Q x x) and not more than 3 controls (counting an ace as 2 controls, a king as 1).

2nd step (2♣) No positive support for spades but upwards of 4 controls.

3rd step (2◇) Positive support (Q x x or better, but not x x x x), not more than 3 controls.

4th step (2♡) Positive support, upwards of 4 controls.

5th step (2♠) 4-card positive support (Q x x x or better), upwards of 4 controls.

Memory-wise, the only uncertainty will be which comes first as between the second step and the third. After 1♣–1♡–1♠ responder holds:

(1)	♠ 5	(2)	♠ K 7 5
	♡ A J 7 4 2		♡ K 9 6 4 3
	◇ A 8 3		◇ K 2
	♣ 9 7 4 2		♣ 8 4 3

The first hand is stronger than the second, but owing to the misfit in spades more space may be needed in which to discover the best contract. On the second hand a good fit is already established, as opener will always have a 5-card suit (otherwise, over a positive, he rebids 1NT). So, the responder can afford to bid one step higher.

The responder may, on occasions, spurn the orthodox responses in order to give a clear picture of his distribution. With a 7-card suit he may jump in his own suit or, more often, with 5-5 or 6-5 he may jump in his second suit. He should not do this with anything better than a singleton in the opener's suit.

After 1♣–1♡ or 1♣–1♠ the opener may rebid 2NT on a 4-3-3-3 minimum hand, 16 or 17 points. This is not an asking bid of any kind. After 1♣–2♣ or 1♣–2◇ opener rebids 2NT on any hand where he was intending to rebid 1NT after 1♣–1◇. This, again, is not an asking bid.

Before examining the continuations after Alpha it is necessary to understand the other types of asking bid.

The Beta bid

A rebid of 1NT after 1♣–1♡ or 1♣–1♠ is Beta, asking for
controls. After 1♣–1♡–1NT responder shows his controls as
follows:

1st step (2♣)   0–2 controls.

2nd step (2◊)   3 controls.

3rd step (2♡)   4 controls.

And so forth.

There is also Beta 4♣. This is a little complicated and can be
left out until the remainder of the scheme has been mastered and
practised.

Beta 4♣ occurs in the following situations:

(a) **When preceded by a major-suit positive, then Alpha
and a reply showing positive support.** The bidding begins:

1♣   1♡
2◊   2NT
4♣

Here the response of 2NT showed positive trump support for
diamonds. 4♣ is Beta, asking for controls. Responder is limited
to 3 controls and he now identifies the exact number as follows:
4◊ 0–1, 4♡ 2, 4♠ 3.

Alternatively, responder may have indicated upper range in his
previous response, as in this sequence:

1♣   1♡
2♣   2NT
4♣

Now responder is known to hold a minimum of 4 controls.
Over 4♣ he bids 4◊ with 4, 4♡ with 5, 4♠ with 6, and so on.

(b) **When preceded by a minor-suit positive, then a
Gamma bid – that is, a raise by opener of his partner's
positive response.** The bidding begins:

1♣   2◊
3◊   3♡
4♣

Opener's 3◇, as we will see in a moment, is Gamma, and the response of 3♡ describes the nature of the diamond suit. Now 4♣ asks for controls, which are shown in the same way as after 1NT Beta: 4◇ 0-2, 4♡ 3, 4♠ 4, and so on.

A slight adjustment has to be made when responder has bid clubs as a natural suit. The bidding begins:

1♣	2♣
3♣	3♡
4◇	

Here 4♣ by opener would be further support for clubs; to ask for controls, via Beta, opener must bid the opposite minor.

The Gamma bid

The third type of asking bid occurs when opener supports his partner's suit. This initiates inquiry about the suit, to which responder answers as follows:

1st step	No top honour (ace, king or queen).
2nd step	5-card suit headed by one honour.
3rd step	5-card suit headed by two honours.
4th step	6-card suit headed by one honour.
5th step	6-card suit headed by two honours.
6th step	Three top honours.

The mnemonic is 012–123.

The sequence 1♣–1NT–2♣

When asking bids are played it is usual to extend the range of the 1NT response from 8–10 to 8–13. Otherwise, whenever responder has 11–13 he has to bid 2NT and the Alpha exchanges begin at an inconveniently high level.

After 1♣–1NT a new suit by opener, apart from 2♣, is normal Alpha. When the opener has a flat minimum he may bid 2NT, but more often he bids 2♣, to which the responses are:

2◇	8–10, no 4-card major.
2♡ 2♤	8–10, four cards in the suit named.
2NT	11–13, no information yet about major suits.

After 1♤–1NT–2♤–2NT opener may bid a suit of his own (not Alpha) or bid 3♤, Baron.

After 1♤–2NT (14 upwards) opener may continue with a new suit (Alpha) or with 3♤ (Baron), or, if you care to remember it, 4♤ (modified Beta, with the first step showing 2–3 controls, the next step 4 controls).

Which sequence to apply

The next question is, which type of asking bid should the opener employ first after the positive response? To this there is both a technical and a tactical answer.

The technical answer is determined by these rules:

1. Alpha is Alpha only if it comes FIRST. You cannot begin with Gamma and follow with Alpha. Take this sequence:

1♤	1♡
2♡ (gamma)	2NT (5-card suit, one honour)
3♤	

As opener did not bid his suit immediately, 3♤ is natural, not requiring Alpha responses.

2. Beta 1NT must occur on the first round, obviously. As explained above, Beta 4♤ occurs when the bidding has begun 1♤–1♡ or 1♤–1♤ and the response to opener's Alpha has shown trump support, or when the bidding has begun 1♤–2♤ or 1♤–2◇ and opener has then used Gamma. The reason for these conditions is that after 1♤–1♡ or 1♤–1♤ opener can always inquire for controls by bidding a Beta 1NT. When you get Alpha followed by Gamma the bidding is usually at the three level already and 4♤ is more likely to be wanted as a cue-bid than as Beta.

3. Gamma may come immediately or it may follow Alpha or Beta 1NT. It cannot follow any natural call. (This is an unvarying rule – once there has been a natural call, asking bids cannot be resumed.) Gamma operates up to the three level, but not beyond.

Thus asking bids can follow one another only in the following sequences:

Alpha–Beta 4♣.
Alpha – Gamma.
Beta 1NT – Gamma.
Gamma in a minor suit – Beta 4♣ (or 4◇ if clubs have been bid).

We turn now to the question of tactics. Suppose the bidding begins 1♣–1♡ and opener holds:

♠ A J 7 5 3
♡ K 7 4
◇ A Q 6
♣ A 5

On the surface he might use Alpha or Beta 1NT or Gamma. But if you reflect that Alpha must come first if at all, it becomes clear that he should begin with Alpha, as partner's holding in spades is certainly important. Suppose the response is 1NT. That tells him two things – no positive support for spades and not more than three controls. However, slam is still not excluded and the next step is 2♡, Gamma. Perhaps partner will bid something cheerful like 3♡, indicating A Q x x x. Opener will then follow with a cue-bid of four clubs, to see what that produces.

Thus it is a general principle that when opener has a broken suit of his own he should begin with Alpha. On the next round 2NT is a very important and useful bid, described as 'shape inquiry'. It asks partner to describe his distribution. The bidding begins:

1♣   1♠
2♣   2 any
2NT

Whatever the response to Alpha has been, 2NT asks for further description. The answer may be a second suit no better than Q x x x, or a rebid in spades, or delayed support for clubs (doubtless x x x or a doubleton honour), or 3NT with 5–3–3–2 and nothing more to say.

When the opener has a more or less solid suit of his own there is less reason for employing Alpha. It will probably be correct now to use Beta 1NT. The bidding begins 1♣–1♡ and the opener holds:

> ♠ A K Q J 9 5
> ♡ K 4
> ◇ A K 5
> ♣ 6 3

Now he wants to get a picture of partner's controls, so he uses Beta 1NT.

It is normal to begin with Beta 1NT on any hand lacking a 5-card suit. The exception occurs on a flat minimum when opener has no top honour in his partner's suit; he may then bid 2NT to indicate general disinterest.

It is not as a rule economical to employ Gamma on the first round after a major-suit response. Remember that you can follow Alpha with Gamma but not Gamma with Alpha. Here is an example from match play:

West	East
♠ 5	♠ A.10 7 4 2
♡ K J 9 7 6 3	♡ A Q 8 5
◇ 7	◇ A 10
♣ A 10 8 6 2	♣ K 4

With East the dealer, the bidding goes:

West	East
	1♣
1♡	1♠ (1)
3♣ (2)	3♡
4◇ (3)	7♡
pass	

(1) Despite his good support for hearts, East follows the normal procedure of beginning with Alpha. Alternatively, he might have begun with Beta 1NT, to be followed by a Gamma raise.

(2) Spurning Alpha, West makes an irregular rebid to give a picture of his 2-suiter. This bid, it may be recalled, is made only with a singleton or void of partner's suit.

(3) The situation is a little unusual, but West treats 3♡ as Gamma and shows a 6-card suit headed by one of the top honours.

The play

A diamond was led against 7♥ and the declarer (who was not in fact a Precision player and had reached 7♥ by a different route) incautiously laid down the ace of hearts at trick two. North showed out, and as South had a doubleton club alongside his 10 7 2 of trumps the declarer was unable to ruff twice and establish the long club. Thus the hand came to a disappointing end. The safe play, easy to miss in the flush of triumph at reaching the grand slam, is to lead a low heart to the jack. Then if South has the three trumps and the doubleton club declarer can ruff twice with the ace and queen; no problem arises if North has the three trumps and the doubleton club.

The effect of intervention

So far as possible, the asking bid structure is maintained in face of intervention. There are two situations to consider – when there is a bid in front of the player who wants to make the asking bid, and when there is intervention in front of the responder. To take the first case, suppose the bidding goes:

South	West	North	East
1♣	pass	2♦	2♠
?			

At this point 3♥ by opener would be Alpha and 3♦ would be Gamma.

The more interesting situation is when there is intervention between the asking bid and the responder, as here:

South	West	North	East
1♣	pass	1♠	2♦
2♥	3♦	?	

Now the schedule for North is as follows:

No positive support and limited controls: Double.
No support but upwards of 4 controls: Pass
Positive support, limited controls: Next suit.

And so on, following the schedule of responses to Alpha. In

other words, Double is the first step, Pass the second step. The same principle is followed when there is intervention between Gamma and the responder:

South	West	North	East
1♣	pass	1♡	1♠
2♡	3♣	?	

South's 2♡ is Gamma and the first step for North, indicating no top honour, is Double, the next Pass, the next 3NT, and so on.

Same, again, when there is intervention over Beta 1NT.

Asking bids retain their character up to the three level but do not operate at the four level.

Use of space

Good bidders, like town and country planners, need to make the best use of the space available. When rounds of bidding are omitted, either there is a tactical reason or a particular inference can be drawn. Sometimes the long way round may not seem necessary. I happened recently to notice this hand from a book I wrote twenty years ago:

West	East
♠ A K J	♠ 10 7 3
♡ A 10 7 2	♡ J 8 4
◇ A Q 8 5 3	◇ K 6
♣ K	♣ A Q J 6 2

A Precision pair, using asking bids, would take the long route, something like this:

West	East
1♣	2♣
2◇	2♡ (1)
2NT (2)	3◇ (3)
3♡	3NT
4♣ (4)	4◇ (5)
4♠	5♣ (6)
6NT	pass

(1) Showing less than Q x x in diamonds and not more than three controls.

149

(2) The standard waiting bid, to learn more about partner's hand.

(3) East takes the opportunity to show that he has secondary support in diamonds.

(4) Both economical and informative.

(5) This conveys that the diamond support is an honour, not three small.

(6) The sign-off at this point would be 4NT. 5♣ shows additional values in the suit.

So there they are, in 6NT, and West, at least, could draw a diagram of his partner's hand.

When the deal first appeared I suggested this Acol sequence:

West	East
1♦	2♣
3NT	4NT
6NT	pass

Also good enough, on this occasion. We used, in those days, to congratulate ourselves on those leaping auctions; but it's not the best way.

The play

North leads a spade against 6NT, giving the declarer a good start. It would be a slight error now to cash the king of clubs and cross to the king of diamonds to run the clubs. Suppose the clubs are 5–2 and the player with the long clubs also has four diamonds; then, when you seek to clear the diamonds, this player will have a club to cash. The safety play is to cash the king of clubs, then duck the *first* round of diamonds; so long as the diamonds are not worse than 4–2 you cannot fail to make four diamonds, four clubs, and four tricks in the majors.

Summary

Asking bids occur only when there is a positive response to 1♣. All rebids except 2NT are asking bids.

When opener bids a new suit over the positive, this is Alpha. Responder replies in five steps: 1, no positive support (Q x x), not more than 3 controls; 2, no positive support, 4 or more controls; 3, positive support, limited controls; 4, positive support, 4 or more controls; 5, 4-card positive support, 4 or more controls. With a strongly distributed hand responder may by-pass the Alpha responses and go beyond the five steps.

When opener rebids 1NT, this is Beta. Responses: 1 step, 0–2 controls, 2 steps 3 controls, and so on.

When opener raises his partner's suit, this is Gamma. Responses in steps: 1, no top honour; 2, 5-card suit with one honour; 3, 5-card suit with two honours; 4, 6-card suit with one honour; 5, 6-card suit with two honours; 6, three top honours.

There is also Beta 4♣. This occurs (a) when there has been a major-suit positive, followed by Alpha and a reply indicating trump support; (b) when there has been a minor-suit positive and an immediate Gamma raise. When clubs have been bid, 4♦ is Beta. Beta 4♣ asks for controls. The responses depend on how many controls the player has already shown. When he is limited to three the responses are 4♦ 0–1, 4♥ 2, 4♠ 3; when he is marked with four or more the responses are 4♦ 4, 4♥ 5, and so on; following the Gamma raise, responses to 4♣ (or 4♦) are on the same lines as over Beta 1NT.

An Alpha bid must always be made at the first opportunity; otherwise the suit is natural. Alpha may be followed by Gamma, by Beta 4♣ in the circumstances described, by a natural bid in another suit, or by 2NT, which is 'shape inquiry'.

Gamma may be bid immediately, or following Alpha or following Beta 1NT.

When there is intervention in front of the player who has opened 1♣, all bids up to the three level retain their character as asking bids. When there is intervention between the asking bidder and the responder, the first step for responder (up to the three level) is double, the next pass, then the next suit, and so on.

21 GETTING RESULTS FROM PRECISION

I must admit to having had occasional qualms about the airy comment in Chapter 1 that the Precision System was easy to learn. There is a lot to learn, I realize, even for players who are accustomed to the language of modern bidding. But the system is logical and coherent; after a while it all fits together in the mind.

There are four stages before you can expect to get results from a new system: you must understand it; you must know it; you must practise it; and you must play it.

You must be sure you understand why the various bids have the sense attributed to them, and what part they play in the general scheme. If you forget for a moment what an opening 2◇ is about, or what are the responses to 2♣, don't remind yourself by looking at the summary: think it out, and then you won't forget again.

The next stage is to know, without effort, the meaning of all the sequences. There is a wrong way, and a right way, to become 'word perfect'. It is useless, when you are doubtful about a sequence, to look through the summary and say 'Yes, of course, I remember that'. You don't know any sequence until you can recall the details *without* looking at the book.

As for practice, C. C. Wei has some good suggestions about this. With permission, I quote from his book introducing the system:

(a) To practise 1♣ bids: deal 13 cards to each player with a pack from which three small cards in each suit have been removed.

(b) To practise major-suit opening bids: deal with a pack from which three small cards in each minor suit have been removed.

(c) To practise 1◇ and 2♣ openings, deal with a pack from which three small cards in each major suit have been removed.

(d) To practise 2◇ opening bids: deal with a pack from which all diamonds have been removed except ace, four, three, and two.

(e) For practice with freak hands: use a full pack and deal goulash fashion without shuffling, five cards to each player, then five again and finally three.

To which I would add: don't forget to practise bidding over

intervention. Assume, before you and your partner pick up your cards, that a defender is going to overcall in spades.

Finally, you have to play the system, preferably as a team of four. Don't expect to do great things in your first season. Have trust in the system; when you get a poor result and the Precision method seems to be to blame, don't make fussy changes. If you know the system and play it well you will get the results. The successes won by Precision teams throughout the world are proof of that.

The 'Precision Club'

If you have enjoyed this book and wish to keep in touch with technical developments you may like to join the 'Precision Club', an informal association of players interested in learning and playing the system. The Club publishes a quarterly bulletin, edited by Terence Reese, in which points of theory are discussed. For details, please write to Mrs A. M. Hiron, Hon. Sec. the Precision Club, 25 Baron's Keep, Gliddon Road, London W.14.

STAR BOOKS

are available through all good
booksellers but, where difficulty is encountered,
titles can usually be obtained *by post* from:

Star Book Service,
G.P.O. Box 29,
Douglas,
Isle of Man,
British Isles.

1 or 2 books – retail price + 5p. each copy
3 or more books – retail price post free.

Customers outside Britain should include 7p.
postage and packing for every book ordered.